celebrating CUPCAKES AND MUFFINS

By

Michal Moses

A LEISURE ARTS PUBLICATION

the art of everyday living

Vice President and Chief Operations Officer: Tom Siebenmorgen
Vice President, Sales and Marketing: Pam Stebbins
Vice President, Operations: Jim Dittrich
Editor in Chief: Susan White Sullivan
Director of Designer Relations: Debra Nettles
Senior Art Director: Rhonda Shelby
Senior Prepress Director: Mark Hawkins

Produced for Leisure Arts, Inc. by Penn Publishing Ltd.
www.penn.co.il
Editor: Shoshana Brickman
Design and layout: Ariane Rybski
Photography by: Danya Weiner

PRINTED IN THE U.S.A.

ISBN-13: 978-1-57486-032-0
ISBN-10: 1-57486-032-1
Library of Congress Control Number: 2009930565

Cover photography by Danya Weiner

I would like to dedicate this book:
First and foremost to my parents (the world's best) with love and great gratitude.
To my two amazing brothers and their families, who I am so fortunate to have.
And last but not least to Kish, Shabluli and little Nini.

Thanks to Galit Ries for the sugar decoration on Easter Egg and Bunny Cupcakes and Sweet and Scary Cupcakes.

Contents

Introduction

Cupcakes and muffins are single-serving treats that allow each and every person to have a personalized, delicious, and delightful baked good. They are easy to make, easy to decorate, and can be used to celebrate any type of occasion. They can be prepared in colorful liners, filled with rich creamy fillings, and served almost straight out of the oven. And they usually take just minutes to prepare.

Cupcakes are generally sweeter than muffins and served as dessert. They can be topped with creamy frostings, filled with rich fillings, and decorated any way you like. I like to think of cupcakes a little bit like hugs, only sweeter. They are a unique way to touch someone special and make them feel terrific. Cupcakes are excellent outlets for creativity, too. They can be decorated with a wide variety of sweet toppings that are homemade, store-bought, or a combination of the two. Cupcakes are perfect for serving at outdoor parties, picnics, and other occasions. You can decorate them in advance or invite your guests to help, which is particularly fun when the occasion includes children!

Muffins may be sweet or savory and are often served warm. They are a type of quick bread, leavened with baking powder and soda rather than yeast. You can serve muffins at breakfast, brunch, or lunch, with jam and butter or alongside soups and salads. Muffins are popular between-meal snacks, too, and are excellent for staving off hunger or satisfying a craving. Both muffins and cupcakes are easy to make and require simple ingredients and tools that can be found in most home kitchens.

In **Celebrating Cupcakes and Muffins**, you'll find a wide variety of recipes for muffins, cupcakes, fillings, and frostings that are perfect for turning any ordinary occasion into an extra special event. There are also dozens of ideas for assembling these sweet treats and making them as beautiful as they are tasty. I hope these recipes inspire you to create your own designs and use your imagination to mix and match batters, frostings, and fillings.

About the Author

Author Michal Moses is an experienced chef, food writer, and lover of all things culinary. She studied at the "Cordon Bleu" in France, and graduated with a "Grand Diplome" in cooking and pastry. Michal has trained in restaurants in Europe, the United States, and Israel, and has taken continuing education course at the "Culinary Institute of America". Michal's passion for cupcakes dates back to when she visited London as a young girl, and tasted her first, unforgettable, chocolate cupcake.

Basic Recipes

Devil's Food Cupcakes

This cupcake is simple to make, but the flavor is rich and indulgent. A favorite among kids and adults alike, all of its chocolate flavor comes from the cocoa!

INGREDIENTS

Makes 12 cupcakes

¼ cup unsweetened cocoa powder

¼ cup boiling water

½ stick (2 ounces) unsalted butter, softened

¾ cup sugar

1 large egg

1 teaspoon pure vanilla extract

1¼ cups all-purpose flour

¾ teaspoon baking soda

Pinch of salt

¾ cup buttermilk

PREPARATION

1. Preheat oven to 350°F and line a standard cupcake pan with paper liners.

2. In a small cup, mix together cocoa powder and boiling water until cocoa dissolves. Set aside to cool.

3. In the bowl of an electric mixer, cream butter and sugar until fluffy and smooth. Add egg and beat well. Mix in vanilla and cooled cocoa until combined.

4. In a separate bowl, sift together flour, baking soda, and salt.

5. Add flour mixture to butter mixture gradually, alternating with buttermilk and beating on very low speed just until batter forms. Take care not to over mix.

6. Spoon batter into cupcake cups, filling each cup about two-thirds full.

7. Bake for about 15 minutes, or until a toothpick inserted in the center comes out clean.

8. Transfer pan to a wire rack and let cupcakes cool to room temperature.

9. Frost as desired and serve immediately, or store in an airtight container and refrigerate for up to 2 days.

Golden Sour Cream Cupcakes

This basic recipe has the right amount of light, airy sweetness. If you don't have sour cream, substitute with buttermilk. If you don't have buttermilk, place 1 teaspoon fresh lemon juice in a cup, and fill halfway with whole milk. Wait about 15 minutes, until the milk curdles.

INGREDIENTS

Makes 12 cupcakes

1 stick (4 ounces) unsalted butter, softened

1 cup sugar

1/8 teaspoon pure vanilla or almond extract

2 large eggs

1 1/2 cups all-purpose flour

1 1/2 teaspoons baking powder

Pinch of salt

1/2 cup sour cream or buttermilk

PREPARATION

1. Preheat oven to 350°F and line a standard cupcake pan with paper liners.

2. In the bowl of an electric mixer, cream butter and sugar until fluffy and smooth. Add vanilla; then add eggs one at a time, beating well after each addition.

3. In a separate bowl, sift together flour, baking powder, and salt.

4. Add flour mixture to butter mixture gradually, alternating with sour cream and beating on very low speed until just blended. Take care not to over mix.

5. Spoon batter into cupcake cups, filling each cup about two-thirds full.

6. Bake for about 20 minutes, or until a toothpick inserted in the center comes out clean. Transfer pan to a wire rack and cool cupcakes to room temperature.

7. Frost as desired and serve immediately, or store in an airtight container and refrigerate for up to 2 days.

Triple Chocolate Cupcakes

With cocoa powder, melted chocolate, and chocolate chips, these cupcakes will satisfy any chocolate craving. They are also wonderfully easy to make.

INGREDIENTS

Makes 12 cupcakes

1¼ sticks (5 ounces) unsalted butter, softened

⅔ cup sugar

3 large eggs

2½ ounces dark or milk chocolate, melted

1⅓ cups self-rising flour

2 tablespoons unsweetened cocoa powder

¾ cup semi-sweet chocolate chips

PREPARATION

1. Preheat oven to 350°F and line a standard cupcake pan with paper liners.

2. In the bowl of an electric mixer, cream butter and sugar until fluffy and smooth. Add eggs gradually, beating well after each addition. Mix in melted chocolate.

3. Fold in flour and cocoa powder until just blended. Take care not to over mix. Gently fold in chocolate chips.

4. Spoon batter into cupcake cups, filling each cup about three-quarters full.

5. Bake for 15 to 17 minutes, or until a toothpick inserted in the center comes out clean.

6. Transfer pan to a wire rack and let cupcakes cool to room temperature.

7. Frost as desired and serve immediately, or store in an airtight container and refrigerate for up to 2 days.

Vanilla Chocolate Chip Cupcakes

Can't decide whether you want chocolate or vanilla? These cupcakes are an excellent compromise. For a colorful alternative, replace the chocolate chips with rainbow chips!

INGREDIENTS

Makes 12 cupcakes

1¼ stick (5 ounces) unsalted butter, softened

¾ cup sugar

1 teaspoon pure vanilla extract

3 large eggs

1½ cups all-purpose flour

1½ teaspoons baking powder

⅛ teaspoon salt

4 tablespoons buttermilk

½ cup semi-sweet chocolate chip

PREPARATION

1. Preheat oven 350°F and line a standard cupcake pan with paper liners.

2. In the bowl of an electric mixer, cream butter and sugar until fluffy and smooth. Add vanilla and eggs, one at a time, beating well after each addition.

3. In a separate bowl, sift together flour, baking powder, and salt.

4. Add flour mixture to butter mixture gradually, alternating with buttermilk and beating on very low speed just until batter forms. Take care not to over mix. Gently fold in chocolate chips.

5. Spoon batter into cupcake cups, filling each cup about two-thirds full.

6. Bake for 15 to 20 minutes, or until a toothpick inserted in the center comes out clean.

7. Transfer pan to a wire rack and let cupcakes cool to room temperature.

8. Frost as desired and serve immediately, or store in an airtight container and refrigerate for up to 2 days.

Buttercream Frosting

This delicious frosting is remarkably easy to make and can be whipped up while your cupcakes are cooling. Be sure to use butter that is soft but not melted for this recipe.

INGREDIENTS

Makes about 1½ cups

1 stick (4 ounces) unsalted butter, softened

2 cups confectioner's sugar

2 tablespoons whole milk

Pinch of salt

1 teaspoon pure vanilla extract, to taste

Gel food coloring, optional

PREPARATION

1. In the bowl of an electric mixer, cream butter and 1 cup confectioner's sugar until smooth and fluffy.

2. Add remaining confectioner's sugar and beat until smooth. Add milk, salt, vanilla, and food coloring, and beat until creamy.

3. Use immediately or refrigerate in an airtight container for up to 3 days. When using refrigerated cream, let it sit at room temperature for about 20 minutes and then beat on low speed until creamy.

Chocolate Buttercream Frosting

Dissolve 2 tablespoons unsweetened cocoa powder in 2 tablespoons boiling water. Let the dissolved cocoa cool; then blend in with the milk in step 2 of the Buttercream Frosting recipe. For a rich brown color, add a few drops of red gel food coloring.

Orange Buttercream Frosting

Blend 1 tablespoon finely grated orange zest and a few drops of orange extract with the milk in step 2 of the Buttercream Frosting recipe. To enrich the orange color, add a few drops of orange gel food coloring.

Cream Cheese Frosting

The amount of sugar you use in this recipe depends on your sweet tooth. If you like frosting that is really sweet, gradually add up to 1 additional cup of sugar. Adding sour cream balances and highlights the sweetness.

INGREDIENTS

Makes about 2 cups

8 ounces cream cheese, softened but still cool

5 tablespoons unsalted butter, softened but still cool

1½ teaspoons pure vanilla extract

2 cups confectioner's sugar

1 tablespoon sour cream, optional

PREPARATION

1. In the bowl of an electric mixer, combine cream cheese, butter, and vanilla until smooth.

2. Add the sugar and sour cream, beating until smooth. Use immediately or refrigerate in an airtight container for up to 3 days. When using refrigerated cream, let it sit at room temperature for about 20 minutes and then beat on low speed until creamy.

Chocolate Cream Cheese Frosting

Dissolve 1 tablespoon unsweetened cocoa powder in 1 tablespoon boiling water. Let the dissolved cocoa cool; then blend in with the sour cream in step 2 of the Cream Cheese Frosting recipe.

Royal Icing: Traditional

This classic icing creates a firm, sweet glaze that is very easy to apply. The traditional recipe uses fresh egg whites, but I recommend pasteurized egg whites instead to avoid the risk of salmonella poisoning. You can also use meringue power (see recipe on opposite page). Royal icing hardens quickly when exposed to air, so keep it in a covered container as you work with it. You can also add a few drops of glycerin to prevent the icing from hardening.

INGREDIENTS

Makes about 2 cups

¼ cup pasteurized liquid egg whites (equivalent to 2 large egg whites)

1½ tablespoons teaspoons fresh lemon juice

3 cups confectioner's sugar

Gel food coloring, optional

Flavor extract, optional

PREPARATION

1. In the bowl of an electric mixer, beat egg whites and lemon juice until frothy. Add sugar gradually while beating on medium speed until mixture is smooth and shiny.

2. Increase mixer speed to high, and beat for about 5 minutes, until stiff glossy peaks form and mixture is stable enough to glaze a cupcake.

3. To check consistency, dip a spoon in the glaze and draw it upward, letting a bit fall back into the bowl. If the glaze can be seen on the surface of the mixture for 5 to 7 seconds, the icing is ready.

4. If the mixture is still a bit runny, beat in more sugar and test again.

5. Add food coloring and extract as desired, and use immediately.

Royal Icing: With Meringue Powder

In this recipe, the liquid egg whites are substituted with meringue powder, made from dry egg whites and flavoring. Meringue powder eliminates the risks associated with raw egg whites, and it is an excellent alternative when serving young children, elderly people, or anyone with a compromised immune system.

INGREDIENTS

Makes about 2½ cups

4 cups confectioner's sugar

3 tablespoons meringue powder

⅓ to ⅔ cup warm water

Gel food coloring, optional

Flavor extract, optional

PREPARATION

1. In the bowl of an electric mixer, combine sugar and meringue powder.

2. Add water gradually while beating, until stiff glossy peaks form and mixture is stable enough to glaze a cupcake.

3. To check consistency, dip a spoon in the glaze and draw it upward, letting a bit fall back into the bowl. If the glaze can be seen on the surface of the mixture for 5 to 7 seconds, the icing is ready.

4. If the mixture is still a bit runny, beat in more sugar and test again.

5. Add food coloring and extract, as desired, and use immediately.

Confectioner's Sugar Glaze

This icing takes just a few seconds to make, doesn't require any eggs, milk, or butter, and tops cupcakes with a fine matte glaze. It's perfect for kids who want to help decorate, and they can choose the color.

INGREDIENTS

Makes about 1 cup

1 cup confectioner's sugar

1 tablespoon warm water

Gel food coloring, optional

PREPARATION

1. Place sugar in a small bowl. Add water gradually, and mix until smooth. Icing is the right consistency when it is thick enough to coat the back of a spoon. Add more water or sugar, as required.

2. Mix in a few drops of food coloring until desired shade is achieved. Use immediately.

Lemon or Lime Confectioner's Sugar Glaze

Replace the water in the basic recipe with 1 tablespoon lemon or lime juice. After the glaze is smooth, mix in 1 teaspoon finely grated lemon or lime zest, and a bit of green or yellow gel food coloring.

Chocolate Ganache Glaze

Ganache is the French term for a rich icing or filling made from heated cream and chocolate. This version is easy to make and results in a smooth, shiny cupcake topping. It also happens to be utterly delicious! The secret to a really shiny ganache glaze is taking care not to overheat the chocolate. I recommend pouring the boiled cream over the chopped chocolate pieces to melt them.

INGREDIENTS

Makes 2½ cups

10 ounces dark or milk chocolate, chopped into small pieces

¾ cup heavy (whipping) cream

4 tablespoons corn syrup

3 tablespoons unsalted butter, softened

PREPARATION

1. Place chocolate in a large heatproof bowl and set aside.

2. Place cream in a small pot and bring to a boil over medium-high heat.

3. Remove cream from heat and pour over chocolate immediately. Let stand for 5 minutes; then mix gently until creamy and smooth.

4. Add corn syrup and butter, mixing until smooth. Use immediately or refrigerate in an airtight container until needed. Gently reheat until smooth before using.

Custard Filling

Known as crème patisserie in French, this thickened vanilla cream will dramatically upgrade any cupcake with a rich, sweet filling. If you've never made custard from scratch, now is the time to try. It's easier than you might imagine, and tastier as well. For a really scrumptious treat, mix ½ cup whipped cream into the custard just before serving. Note that the eggs are poached but not fully cooked, a possible health concern for people with challenged immune systems.

INGREDIENTS

Makes about 1½ cups

1 whole egg

2 large egg yolks

4 tablespoons sugar

3 tablespoons cornstarch

1 cup whole milk

½ vanilla bean, split lengthwise, or 1 teaspoon natural vanilla extract

PREPARATION

1. In a small heatproof bowl, vigorously whisk egg, egg yolks, and sugar until mixture is pale in color. Add cornstarch and mix until fully blended.

2. In a small saucepan, heat milk and vanilla over medium-high heat until mixture just comes to a boil.

3. Add half the milk to egg mixture, and mix until smooth.

4. Pour egg mixture through a fine metal sieve back into the saucepan, and cook over medium-low heat, whisking constantly, until cream thickens.

5. Continue to cook for another 2 minutes, whisking constantly so that custard doesn't stick to bottom of saucepan.

6. Remove custard from heat and pour into a shallow flat tray. Cover with plastic wrap, making sure the plastic touches the surface of the custard to prevent a crust from forming.

7. Refrigerate for at least 20 minutes, or up to 2 days.

Lemon Curd Filling

This tangy cream will tickle your palate and give your cupcakes a creamy, moist center. Be sure to use freshly squeezed lemon juice for the best flavor, and remember that the eggs are poached but not fully cooked, out of concern for people with challenged immune systems.

INGREDIENTS

Makes about 2 cups

4 large eggs

1¼ cups sugar

10 tablespoons freshly squeezed lemon juice

2 tablespoons finely grated lemon zest

2 sticks (8 ounces) unsalted butter, softened and cut into small pieces

PREPARATION

1. Place eggs, sugar, lemon juice, and lemon zest in a heatproof bowl. Place bowl on a pot containing about 2 inches of water, and place pot on low heat. Make sure bottom of bowl does not come in contact with simmering water.

2. Whisk mixture constantly for 10 to 15 minutes, until it thickens into a cream. Remove bowl from heat and let mixture cool at room temperature for about 10 minutes.

3. Whisk butter gradually into cream mixture until fully blended. Refrigerate for least 2 hours, until curd is thoroughly chilled and stabilized.

Orange Curd Filling

Replace lemon juice in Lemon Curd Filling recipe with freshly squeezed orange juice, and replace lemon zest with orange zest. You can reduce the amount of sugar to 1 cup since orange juice is sweeter than lemon juice.

Whipped Chocolate Ganache Filling

This decadent filling is made with just two ingredients but is rich and flavorful. It must be refrigerated a day in advance, which requires a bit of planning but ultimately cuts down your overall preparation time.

INGREDIENTS

Makes about 1½ cups

5½ ounces dark or milk chocolate, chopped into small pieces

1½ cups heavy (whipping) cream

PREPARATION

1. Place chocolate in a small heatproof bowl and set aside.

2. Place cream in a small pot and bring to a boil over medium-high heat.

3. Remove cream from heat and pour over chocolate immediately. Let stand for 5 minutes; then whisk until creamy and smooth. Let mixture cool to room temperature, cover with plastic wrap, and refrigerate overnight.

4. Just before serving, whip cold ganache until light and airy using an electric hand blender or whisk. Take care not to over mix since this can cause the cream to separate.

Whipped White Chocolate Ganache Filling

For an even more decadent filling, replace the dark or milk chocolate in the Whipped Chocolate Ganache Filling recipe with 6 ounces white chocolate, and use a full cup of cream. You can also add 1 or 2 teaspoons of orange liqueur, orange extract, or grated orange zest in step 3.

Say It With Cupcakes

Real Flower Cupcakes

•

Sugar 'n' Spice (and Everything Nice)

•

Orange Cupcakes

•

Superstar Cupcakes

•

Bananas about You!

•

Country Wedding Cupcakes

•

Gingerbread Cupcakes

•

Banana Chocolate Chip Cupcakes

•

Swirled Orange Brownie Cupcakes

•

Strawberry Cheesecakes

•

Lemon Cupcakes

•

Raspberry Marbled Vanilla Cupcakes

•

Toffee-Topped Banana Cupcakes

•

Little Lemon Meringues

•

White Rose Cupcakes

•

Pecan Banana Cupcakes

•

Lemon Lime Cupcakes

•

Garden of Flowers Cupcakes

•

Cocoa Nutty Mountain Cupcakes

Real Flower Cupcakes

Fresh flowers are used to mark many special occasions. Why not use them to decorate cupcakes, too? Make sure you buy edible flowers that were grown without pesticides.

INGREDIENTS

Makes 12 cupcakes

Custard Filling (page 19)

Vanilla Chocolate Chip Cupcakes (page 11)

Cream Cheese Frosting (page 13)

Edible flowers, such as pansies or snap dragons

PREPARATION

1. Prepare filling and refrigerate until ready to use.

2. Prepare cupcakes and cool completely.

3. Transfer chilled filling to a piping bag fitted with a round tip or to a squeeze bottle.

4. Insert tip into center of each cupcake and pipe in about 1 tablespoon of filling.

5. Prepare frosting, and spread generously on cupcake tops using a palette or flat knife.

6. Sprinkle with flower petals and serve immediately.

Sugar 'n' Spice (and Everything Nice)

Awaken taste buds with a tangy and tart topping for the sweet gingerbread cupcakes. If you're not crazy about candied ginger, top with candied orange zest.

INGREDIENTS

Makes 12 cupcakes

Orange Curd Filling (page 20)

Gingerbread Cupcakes (page 34)

Orange Buttercream Frosting (page 12)

⅓ cup candied ginger

PREPARATION

1. Prepare filling and refrigerate for at least 2 hours.

2. Prepare cupcakes and cool completely.

3. Transfer chilled filling to a piping bag fitted with a round tip or to a squeeze bottle.

4. Insert tip into center of each cupcake and pipe in about 1 tablespoon of filling.

5. Prepare frosting, and spread generously on cupcake tops using a palette or flat knife.

6. Top with candied ginger and serve.

Orange Cupcakes

With orange zest and freshly squeezed orange juice, these cupcakes are moist, fragrant, and flavorful. They don't rise very much during baking, which gives you a flat surface that is perfect for decorating.

INGREDIENTS

Makes 18 cupcakes

1 stick (4 ounces) unsalted butter

1 cup sugar

2 large eggs

1 tablespoon finely grated orange zest (from 2 oranges)

1½ cups all-purpose flour

1½ teaspoons baking powder

1 cup whole milk

½ cup freshly squeezed orange juice

PREPARATION

1. Preheat oven to 350°F and line a standard cupcake pan with paper liners.

2. In the bowl of an electric mixer, cream butter and sugar until creamy and airy.

3. Add orange zest and eggs, one at a time, beating well after each addition.

4. In a separate bowl, sift together flour and baking powder.

5. Add flour mixture to butter mixture gradually, alternating with milk and orange juice, and beating on very low speed just until batter forms.

6. Spoon batter into cupcake cups, filling each cup about three-quarters full.

7. Bake for 15 to 20 minutes, or until a toothpick inserted in the center comes out clean.

8. Transfer pan to a wire rack and let cupcakes cool to room temperature.

9. Frost as desired and serve immediately, or store in an airtight container and refrigerate for up to 2 days.

Superstar Cupcakes

Celebrating a school graduation, basketball team win, or top marks on an exam? Express your pride with these special cupcakes for your superstar. Double the batch for a whole bunch of superstars.

INGREDIENTS

Makes 12 cupcakes

Custard Filling (page 19)

Golden Sour Cream Cupcakes (page 9)

¼ cup confectioner's sugar, for dusting

9 ounces red rolled fondant

3 ounces blue rolled fondant

¼ cup jam

PREPARATION

1. Prepare filling and refrigerate until ready to use.

2. Prepare cupcakes and cool completely.

3. Transfer chilled filling to a piping bag fitted with a round tip or to a squeeze bottle. Insert tip into center of each cupcake and pipe in about 1 tablespoon of filling.

4. Dust work surface with confectioner's sugar. Roll out red rolled fondant until it is about ⅛-inch thick.

5. Cut out rounds using 2¾-inch round cutter; then use a star cutter to cut a star from each disc.

6. Repeat to make 12 red discs with star-shaped areas in the center.

7. Roll out blue rolled fondant until it is about ⅛-inch thick; then use a star cutter to cut out 12 stars.

8. Spread cupcake tops with jam and lay red fondant discs on top.

9. Place a blue fondant star into the space in every disc, and serve.

Bananas about You!

This simple cupcake is sure to be a favorite. For pizzazz, use multi-colored silicone cupcake liners.

INGREDIENTS

Makes 12 cupcakes

Banana Chocolate Chip Cupcakes (page 35)

Chocolate Ganache Glaze (page 18)

2 tablespoons black and white jimmies

PREPARATION

1. Prepare cupcakes and cool completely.

2. Prepare glaze. Top each cupcake with a teaspoon of glaze and sprinkle with jimmies.

3. Refrigerate until glaze sets and serve.

Country Wedding Cupcakes

These pretty cupcakes make a lovely and light dessert, perfect for capping off a big festive meal. Make a double or triple batch for serving at an engagement party, anniversary party, or country-style wedding.

INGREDIENTS

Makes 12 cupcakes

Vanilla Chocolate Chip Cupcakes (page 11)

Cream Cheese Frosting (page 13)

2 tablespoons candy pearls

5 sugar roses

PREPARATION

1. Prepare cupcakes and cool completely.

2. Prepare frosting, and spread evenly on cupcake tops using a palette or flat knife.

3. Sprinkle with candy pearls and arrange on a large platter, interspersed with sugar roses.

4. Serve immediately.

Gingerbread Cupcakes

Your house will be filled with an irresistible aroma as these cupcakes bake. Serve with a cup of espresso or a tall glass of milk.

INGREDIENTS

Makes 12 cupcakes

1 stick (4 ounces) unsalted butter, softened

½ cup light brown sugar

3 large eggs

⅓ cup molasses

¼ cup apple juice

1 teaspoon freshly grated ginger

1½ cups all-purpose flour

1 teaspoon baking soda

½ teaspoon salt

1 teaspoon ground ginger

½ teaspoon ground cinnamon

⅛ teaspoon ground cloves

PREPARATION

1. Preheat oven to 350°F and line a standard cupcake pan with paper liners.

2. In the bowl of an electric mixer, cream butter and sugar until fluffy and smooth. Add eggs, one at a time, beating well after each addition. Beat in molasses, apple juice, and grated ginger.

3. In a separate bowl, sift together flour, baking soda, salt, ground ginger, cinnamon, and cloves.

4. Fold flour mixture into butter mixture until just blended. Take care not to over mix.

5. Spoon batter into cupcake cups, filling each cup about three-quarters full.

6. Bake for about 15 minutes, or until a toothpick inserted in the center comes out clean.

7. Transfer pan to a wire rack and let cupcakes cool to room temperature.

8. Frost as desired and serve immediately, or store in an airtight container and refrigerate for up to 2 days.

Banana Chocolate Chip Cupcakes

For really rich banana flavor, use very ripe bananas in this recipe. Bananas with black peels that are too ripe for eating are just right.

INGREDIENTS

Makes 12 cupcakes

2 sticks (8 ounces) unsalted butter, softened

1½ cups light brown sugar

2 large eggs

1 teaspoon pure vanilla extract

4 medium, very ripe bananas, mashed

2 cups plus 2 tablespoons all-purpose flour

1 teaspoon salt

2 teaspoons baking soda

1 cup semi-sweet chocolate chips

PREPARATION

1. Preheat oven to 350°F and line a standard cupcake pan with paper liners.

2. In the bowl of an electric mixer, cream butter and sugar until fluffy and airy. Add eggs, one at a time, beating well after each addition. Beat in vanilla and bananas until combined.

3. In a separate bowl, sift together flour, salt, and baking powder.

4. Fold flour mixture into butter mixture until just blended. Take care not to over mix. Fold in chocolate chips with as few strokes as possible.

5. Spoon batter into cupcake cups, filling each cup two-thirds full.

6. Bake for about 20 minutes, or until a toothpick inserted in the center comes out clean.

7. Transfer pan to a wire rack and let cupcakes cool to room temperature.

8. Frost as desired and serve immediately, or store in an airtight container and refrigerate for up to 2 days.

Swirled Orange Brownie Cupcakes

The orange and chocolate swirl on this cupcake is so attractive that it's a shame to cover it with frosting. For utter indulgence, serve with a scoop of creamy French vanilla ice cream.

INGREDIENTS

Makes 8 cupcakes

Brownie Cupcake Base:

4½ ounces dark chocolate, chopped into small pieces

1 stick (4 ounces) unsalted butter

2 large eggs

¾ cup sugar

½ cup all-purpose flour

Orange Cream Cheese Swirl:

8 ounces cream cheese

¼ cup sugar

½ tablespoon finely grated orange zest (from 1 orange)

1 large egg

½ tablespoon orange extract or liquor

PREPARATION

1. Prepare brownie base: Preheat oven to 300°F and line a standard cupcake pan with paper liners.

2. Place chocolate and butter in the top of a double boiler, and heat over medium heat, mixing constantly until combined. Set aside to cool.

3. Separately, mix together eggs and sugar in a medium bowl. Mix in chocolate mixture; then fold in flour until just blended. Take care not to over mix. Set aside.

4. Prepare cream cheese swirl: In the bowl of an electric mixer, beat cream cheese, sugar, and orange zest until airy and smooth. Beat in egg and orange extract until well blended.

5. Spoon brownie batter evenly into cupcake cups. Place 1 tablespoon cream cheese mixture into each cup, and use a toothpick to swirl.

6. Bake for about 25 minutes, until set. Transfer pan to a wire rack and let cupcakes cool to room temperature.

7. Serve immediately, or store in an airtight container and refrigerate for up to 2 days.

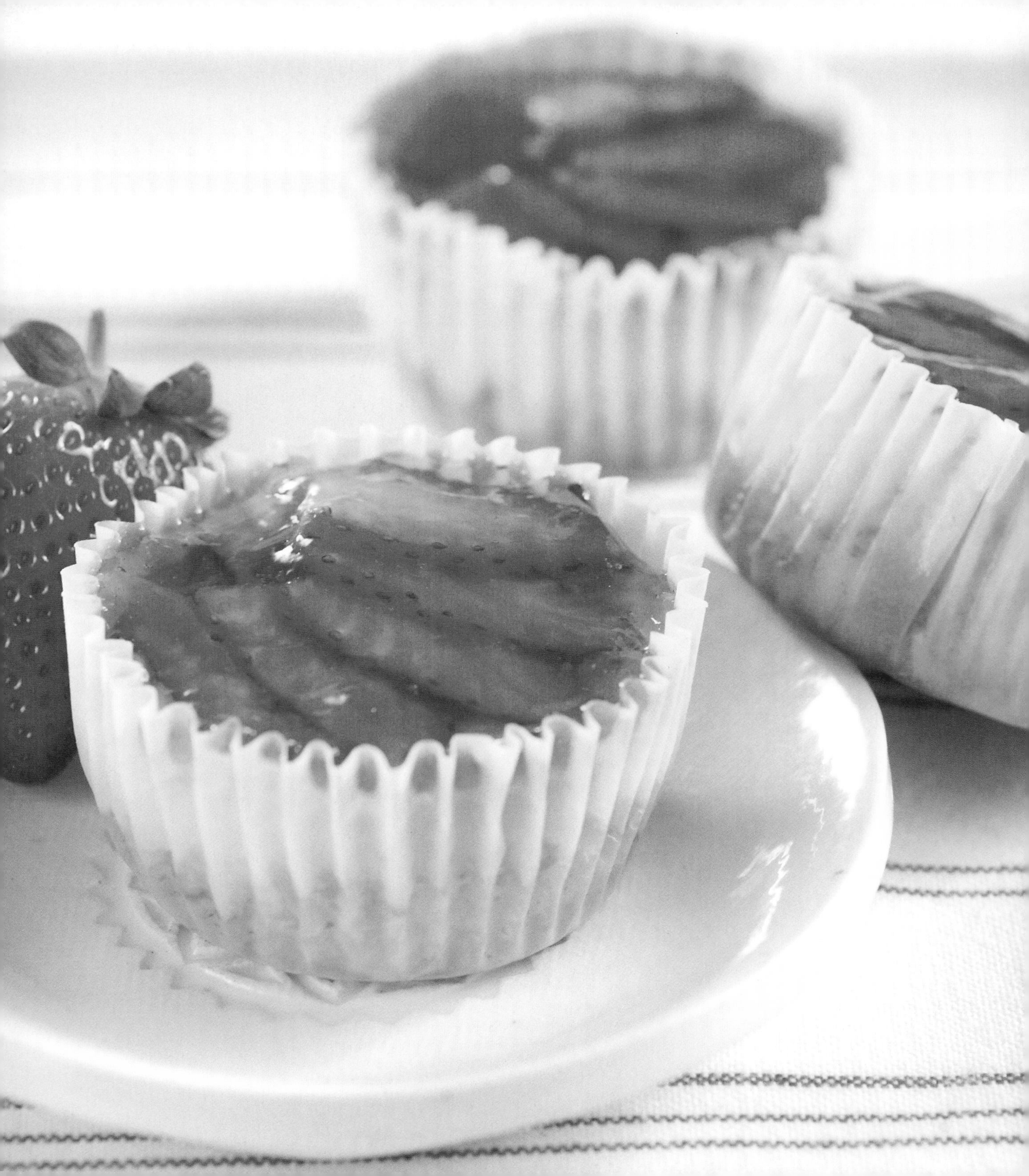

Strawberry Cheesecakes

Delight the guests at your next affair by serving them their very own cheesecakes, topped with a strawberry. These gorgeous cupcakes can also be adorned with fresh blueberries or raspberries.

INGREDIENTS

Makes 12 cupcakes

Cheesecake Cupcakes:
1½ cups crushed graham crackers

8 ounces cream cheese

½ cup sugar

2 large eggs

⅛ teaspoon pure vanilla extract

12 large strawberries, hulled and cut into tiny cubes

Topping:
12 whole strawberries

1 package (¼ ounce) strawberry or raspberry flavored gelatin

PREPARATION

1. Prepare cupcakes: Preheat oven to 350°F and line a standard cupcake pan with paper liners. Press 2 tablespoons crushed graham crackers into base of each paper liner and set aside.

2. In an electric mixer, beat cream cheese, sugar, eggs, and vanilla until smooth. Spoon 2 tablespoons of mixture into each cup and top with cubed strawberries.

3. Bake for about 25 minutes, or until cheesecake sets. Transfer pan to a wire rack and let cupcakes cool to room temperature; then transfer to refrigerator and chill for at least 2 hours.

4. Prepare topping: Slice each strawberry into thin slices, and arrange slices in a fan on cupcake tops.

5. Prepare gelatin according to instructions on package and spoon over cupcakes.

6. Refrigerate for about 20 minutes, until gelatin sets. Serve chilled.

Lemon Cupcakes

This cupcake is a perfect accompaniment to a warm cup of tea. Note that the lemon flavor in this recipe comes entirely from lemon zest. See page 141 for tips on how to grate lemon zest.

INGREDIENTS

Makes 12 cupcakes

1 stick (4 ounces) unsalted butter, melted and cooled to room temperature

2 large eggs

1 cup buttermilk

1 cup sugar

2¼ cups all-purpose flour

1 teaspoon baking powder

1 teaspoon baking soda

2 tablespoons finely grated lemon zest (from 4 lemons)

PREPARATION

1. Preheat oven to 375°F and line a standard cupcake pan with paper liners.

2. In a large bowl, combine butter, eggs, buttermilk, and sugar.

3. In a separate bowl, sift together flour, baking powder, baking soda, and lemon zest.

4. Gradually fold flour mixture into butter mixture just until combined. Take care not to over mix.

5. Spoon batter into cupcake cups, filling each cup about three-quarters full. Bake for about 20 minutes, or until a toothpick inserted in the center comes out clean.

6. Transfer pan to a wire rack and let cupcakes cool to room temperature.

7. Frost as desired and serve immediately, or store in an airtight container and refrigerate for up to 2 days.

Raspberry Marbled Vanilla Cupcakes

Just a touch of raspberry puree transforms a traditional vanilla cupcake into an eye-catching and scrumptious treat.

INGREDIENTS

Makes 12 cupcakes

1 stick (4 ounces) unsalted butter, softened

¾ cup sugar

1 teaspoon pure vanilla extract

3 large eggs

1½ cups all-purpose flour

1½ teaspoons baking powder

3 tablespoons whole milk

⅓ cup raspberries, fresh or frozen and thawed

1 tablespoon sugar

PREPARATION

1. Preheat oven 350°F and line a standard cupcake pan with paper liners.

2. In the bowl of an electric mixer, cream butter and sugar until fluffy and smooth. Add vanilla then eggs, one at a time, beating well after each addition.

3. In a separate bowl, sift together flour and baking powder.

4. Add flour mixture to butter mixture, alternating with milk, and beating on very low speed just until batter forms. Take care not to over mix.

5. Separately, in a blender or food processor, puree raspberries and sugar until smooth.

6. Spoon batter into paper cups. Top each cupcake with a bit of raspberry puree, and use a toothpick to swirl.

7. Bake for 15 to 20 minutes, or until a toothpick inserted in the center comes out dry.

8. Transfer pan to a wire rack and cool to room temperature.

9. Frost as desired and serve immediately, or store in an airtight container and refrigerate for up to 2 days.

Toffee-Topped Banana Cupcakes

With toffee frosting and slices of banana, these cupcakes are perfect for grown-ups and children alike. Omit the nuts in the Pecan Banana Cupcakes if you plan on serving these to young children.

INGREDIENTS

Makes 12 cupcakes

Toffee Glaze:
1 cup sugar

½ cup water

1 cup heavy (whipping) cream

Pecan Banana Cupcakes (page 48)

2 medium ripe bananas, sliced

PREPARATION

1. Prepare glaze: In a small saucepan, combine sugar and water. Bring to a boil over high heat; then continue cooking, without stirring, until sugar browns and caramelizes.

2. Take care not to over cook because burnt caramel is bitter.

3. Remove saucepan from heat, pour in cream, and whisk to combine.

4. Cool mixture to room temperature; then cover with plastic wrap and refrigerate until chilled.

5. Prepare cupcakes and cool completely.

6. Top cupcakes with bananas slices, pour chilled glaze on top, and serve.

Little Lemon Meringues

Treat your guests to individual lemon meringue pies with this delicious recipe. Perfect for afternoon tea, Sunday brunch, or a Sunday dinner grand finale.

INGREDIENTS

Makes 15 cupcakes

Lemon Curd Filling (page 20)

Lemon Lime Cupcakes (page 49) or Lemon Cupcakes (page 40)

Swiss Meringue Buttercream Frosting:
½ cup pasteurized liquid egg whites (equivalent to 4 large egg whites)

1 cup sugar

½ teaspoon salt

4 sticks (16 ounces) unsalted butter, softened and cut into small cubes

1 teaspoon pure vanilla extract

PREPARATION

1. Prepare filling and refrigerate for at least 2 hours.

2. Prepare cupcakes and cool completely.

3. Transfer chilled filling to a piping bag fitted with a round tip or to a squeeze bottle. Insert tip into center of each cupcake and pipe in about 1 tablespoon of filling.

4. Prepare frosting: Place egg whites, sugar, and salt in a heatproof bowl. Place bowl on a pot containing about 2 inches of water, and place pot on low heat. Make sure bottom of bowl does not come in contact with simmering water.

5. Whisk egg whites and sugar while gently heating until a candy thermometer inserted into the mixture reaches 160°F. (At this temperature, the mixture will be too hot to touch.) Remove bowl from heat.

6. Transfer mixture to the bowl of an electric mixer, or use a hand blender fitted with a whisk attachment, and whisk mixture on high speed for 5 to 7 minutes, until a stiff-peaked and shiny meringue forms. Gradually add butter cubes while whisking until butter blends in fully. Whisk in vanilla.

7. Transfer frosting to a piping bag fitted with a star pastry tip, and frost cupcake tops with little swirls of frosting. Serve immediately.

White Rose Cupcakes

Prepare the filling a day in advance, and whip it just before serving. When piping on the frosting, start in the center and work your way outward.

INGREDIENTS

Makes 12 cupcakes

Whipped White Chocolate Ganache Filling (page 21)

Raspberry Marbled Vanilla Cupcakes (page 41)

White Chocolate Frosting:
5½ ounces white chocolate, chopped into small pieces

⅔ cup heavy (whipping) cream

2 sticks (8 ounces) unsalted butter, softened

1½ cups confectioner's sugar

1 teaspoon orange liqueur, optional

1 tablespoon pink sugar crystals

PREPARATION

1. Prepare filling and chill overnight.

2. Prepare cupcakes and cool completely.

3. Transfer chilled filling to a piping bag fitted with a round tip or to a squeeze bottle. Insert tip into center of each cupcake and pipe in about 1 tablespoon of filling.

4. Prepare frosting: Place chocolate in a small heatproof bowl and set aside. Place cream in a small pot and bring to a boil over medium-high heat.

5. Remove cream from heat and pour over chocolate immediately. Let sit for about 5 minutes; then whisk until creamy and smooth.

6. Strain out any pieces of chocolate that haven't melted, and refrigerate the rest until completely cold. If you are in a hurry, place in the freezer for a few minutes.

7. In the meantime, in the bowl of an electric mixer, cream butter and sugar until airy and smooth. Beat in chilled chocolate cream mixture until smooth. Beat in liqueur until blended.

8. Transfer frosting to a piping bag fitted with a star tip, and pipe frosting in a rose shape on top of each cupcake. Sprinkle with sugar crystals and serve immediately.

Pecan Banana Cupcakes

The pecans in these cupcakes can be replaced with walnuts if you like. As for the cardamom, it can be replaced with cinnamon for a different flavor and aroma.

INGREDIENTS

Makes 12 cupcakes

2 sticks (8 ounces) unsalted butter, softened

1½ cups sugar

2 large eggs

2 cups plus 2 tablespoons all-purpose flour

2 teaspoons baking soda

¼ teaspoon ground cardamom or cinnamon

1 teaspoon salt

1 cup chopped pecans or walnuts

16 ounces (about 3 to 4 medium) very ripe bananas, mashed

PREPARATION

1. Preheat oven to 350°F and line a standard cupcake pan with paper liners.

2. In the bowl of an electric mixer, cream butter and sugar until fluffy and smooth. Add eggs, one at a time, beating well after each addition. Beat in mashed bananas until combined.

3. In a separate bowl, sift together flour, baking soda, cardamom, and salt.

4. Gently fold flour mixture into butter mixture until just blended. Take care not to over mix. Fold in pecans with as few strokes as possible.

5. Spoon batter into cupcake cups, filling each cup two-thirds full. Bake for about 20 minutes, or until a toothpick inserted in the center comes out clean.

6. Transfer pan to a wire rack and cool to room temperature.

7. Frost as desired and serve immediately, or store in an airtight container and refrigerate for up to 2 days.

Lemon Lime Cupcakes

This bright cupcake sparkles with lemon and lime zest. It's perfect for afternoon tea when topped with Lemon or Lime Confectioner's Sugar Glaze (page 16).

INGREDIENTS

Makes 15 cupcakes

4 large eggs

1 cup sugar

1¾ cups self-rising flour

8 ounces (2 sticks) unsalted butter, melted and cooled to room temperature

2 tablespoons whole milk

1 tablespoon finely grated lemon zest (from 2 lemons)

1 tablespoon finely grated lime zest (from 2 limes)

PREPARATION

1. Preheat oven to 350°F and line a standard cupcake pan with paper liners.

2. In the bowl of an electric mixer, beat eggs and sugar until airy and fluffy.

3. Add flour, butter, milk, lemon zest, and lime zest, and beat on slow speed until just blended.

4. Spoon batter into cupcake cups, filling each cup about two-thirds full. Bake for about 15 minutes, or until a toothpick inserted in the center comes out clean.

5. Transfer pan to a wire rack and let cupcakes cool to room temperature.

6. Frost as desired and serve immediately, or store in an airtight container and refrigerate for up to 2 days.

Garden of Flowers Cupcakes

These pretty cupcakes are easy to make if you use prepared sugar flowers. If you'd like to try your hand at making your own flowers, go right ahead!

INGREDIENTS

Makes 12 cupcakes

Custard Filling (page 19)

Vanilla Chocolate Chip Cupcakes (page 11)

Royal Icing (page 14)

Purple, pink, yellow, and green pastel gel food coloring

12 edible sugar flowers

PREPARATION

1. Prepare filling, and refrigerate until ready to use.

2. Prepare cupcakes and cool completely.

3. Transfer chilled filling to a piping bag fitted with a round tip or to a squeeze bottle.

4. Insert tip into center of each cupcake and pipe in about 1 tablespoon of filling.

5. Prepare icing and tint as desired. Top each cupcake with 1 teaspoon icing, and place a sugar flower in center before icing sets.

6. Set aside until icing sets and serve.

Cocoa Nutty Mountain Cupcakes

Love chocolate? These cupcakes feature a chocolate base, smooth chocolatey center, creamy chocolate frosting, and chocolate-coated almond topping. Prepare the filling a day in advance, and whip it just before serving. The almond clusters can be prepared several days in advance.

INGREDIENTS

Makes 24 mini cupcakes

Whipped Chocolate Ganache Filling (page 21)

Almond Clusters:
1 cup slivered almonds

2½ ounces dark chocolate, chopped into small pieces

¼ cup unsweetened cocoa powder

Devil's Food Cupcakes (page 8)

Chocolate Buttercream Frosting (page 12)

PREPARATION

1. Prepare filling and chill overnight.

2. Prepare clusters: Preheat oven to 300°F. Spread almonds on a baking sheet and toast for about 7 minutes, until golden. Transfer to a heatproof bowl and set aside to cool. Line a baking sheet with parchment paper.

3. Melt chocolate in the top of a double boiler. Pour melted chocolate over almonds and mix until almonds are evenly coated.

4. Pile small clusters of coated almonds on lined baking sheet, and set aside until chocolate solidifies. Dust with cocoa powder.

5. Prepare cupcakes in a mini cupcake pan and cool completely.

6. Transfer chilled filling to a piping bag fitted with a round tip or to a squeeze bottle. Insert tip into center of each cupcake and pipe in about 1 tablespoon of filling.

7. Prepare frosting, and spread generously on cupcakes tops using a palette or flat knife. Place an almond cluster in the center of each cupcake and serve.

Cupcakes For The Calendar

New Year's Eve Cupcakes

•

Red Velvet Cupcakes

•

Snowy Tree Christmas Cupcakes

•

Super Bowl Cupcakes

•

Peanut Cornmeal Cupcakes

•

Cinnamon Heart Cupcakes

•

Easter Egg and Bunny Cupcakes

•

Fourth of July Cupcakes

•

Fresh Pumpkin Cupcakes

•

Sweet and Scary Cupcakes

•

Spooky Spider Web Cupcakes

•

Thanksgiving Cupcakes

New Year's Eve Cupcakes

Celebrating New Year's with your kids? Preparing cupcakes together and eating them at midnight (or a few hours earlier) is a tasty and fun way of ringing in the new year.

INGREDIENTS

Makes 12 cupcakes

Triple Chocolate Cupcakes (page 10)

Chocolate Buttercream Frosting (page 12)

2 tablespoons silver dragées

12 sparklers

PREPARATION

1. Prepare cupcakes and cool completely.

2. Prepare frosting, and spread on cupcakes using a palette or flat knife.

3. Sprinkle silver dragées over cupcakes, insert a sparkler in the center of each, and serve.

Red Velvet Cupcakes

These cupcakes have a dramatic look, thanks to a few drops of red food coloring added to the chocolate batter. To achieve a rich, smooth color, I recommend gel food coloring.

INGREDIENTS

Makes 12 cupcakes

1½ sticks (6 ounces) unsalted butter, softened

2 cups sugar

1 teaspoon pure vanilla extract

1 teaspoon apple vinegar

2 large eggs

2 to 3 tablespoons red food coloring gel

2½ cups all-purpose flour

1 teaspoon baking soda

Pinch of salt

3 teaspoons unsweetened cocoa powder

1 cup buttermilk

PREPARATION

1. Preheat oven to 350°F and line a standard cupcake pan with paper liners.

2. In the bowl of an electric mixer, cream butter and sugar until fluffy and smooth. Mix in vanilla and vinegar; then add eggs, one at a time, beating well after each addition. Gradually add food coloring until desired color is achieved.

3. In a separate bowl, sift together flour, baking soda, salt, and cocoa.

4. Add flour mixture to butter mixture gradually, alternating with buttermilk, and beating on very low speed just until batter forms. Add more food coloring, if necessary. Take care not to over mix.

5. Spoon batter into cupcake cups, filling each cup about two-thirds full.

6. Bake for about 15 minutes, or until a toothpick inserted in the center comes out clean.

7. Transfer pan to a wire rack and let cupcakes cool to room temperature.

8. Frost as desired and serve, or store in an airtight container and refrigerate for up to 2 days.

Snowy Tree Christmas Cupcakes

Santa will love seeing these treats when he comes down the chimney at midnight. Prepare the filling a day in advance and whip it just before serving. A candy thermometer will help you get the frosting just right. Since the egg whites in the frosting are not completely cooked, use pasteurized liquid egg whites rather than fresh.

INGREDIENTS

Makes 12 cupcakes

Whipped Chocolate Ganache Filling (page 21)

Vanilla Chocolate Chip Cupcakes (page 11)

Swiss Meringue Buttercream Frosting (page 45)

½ cup unsweetened shredded coconut

2 tablespoons red sugar sprinkles

PREPARATION

1. Prepare filling and chill overnight.

2. Prepare cupcakes and cool completely.

3. Transfer chilled filling to a piping bag fitted with a round tip or to a squeeze bottle.

4. Insert tip into center of each cupcake and pipe in about 1 tablespoon of filling.

5. Prepare frosting, and transfer to a piping bag fitted with a star tip.

6. Pipe frosting into a tree-shaped swirl on top of each cupcake.

7. Sprinkle with coconut and sugar sprinkles. Serve immediately.

Super Bowl Cupcakes

This cupcake's distinct combination of sweet and savory flavors is a great complement to the Big Game. Regardless of the final score, it will be a winner!

When cooking the caramel for this recipe, keep a few things in mind. Once the water has evaporated and the sugar begins to cook, don't stir the mixture since this causes the sugar to crystallize and the caramel to become grainy. If you want to soften the caramel after it has hardened, heat it gently in a pot, without adding water. Try not to overcook the caramel, since burnt caramel is quite bitter. A candy thermometer is essential in this recipe.

INGREDIENTS

Makes 12 standard cupcakes or 24 mini cupcakes

Peanut Cornmeal Cupcakes (page 63)

Caramelized Popcorn Topping:
3 cups air-popped popcorn

¾ cup sugar

2 tablespoons water

PREPARATION

1. Prepare cupcakes and cool.

2. Prepare topping: Line a baking sheet with parchment paper and spread popcorn evenly on top.

3. In a small saucepan, combine sugar and water, mixing until sugar dissolves. Mix in corn syrup, butter, and a drop of lemon juice, and heat over medium-high heat until boiling. Do not stir once mixture comes to a boil.

4. Continue cooking, without stirring, until mixture becomes golden brown and a candy thermometer inserted into the mixture reads 275°F.

(continued on next page)

(continued from previous page)

2 tablespoons corn syrup, honey, or maple syrup

1 stick (4 ounces) butter

Lemon juice, to prevent sugar from crystallizing

Peanut Butter Frosting:
2½ sticks (9 ounces) unsalted butter, softened and cut into small cubes

2 cups confectioner's sugar

2 tablespoons whole milk

¼ cup smooth peanut butter, at room temperature

5. Remove caramel from heat and pour over popcorn immediately.

6. Mix gently with a heatproof spoon or wooden spatula, until popcorn is evenly covered. Cool to room temperature; then break into chunks.

7. In the meantime, prepare frosting: In the bowl of an electric mixer, cream butter, sugar, and milk, and beat until smooth and fluffy.

8. Add peanut butter and beat until well blended.

9. Spread frosting on cupcakes using a palette or flat knife.

10. Top each cupcake with a chunk of caramelized popcorn and serve immediately.

Peanut Cornmeal Cupcakes

The mild sweetness of these cupcakes is offset by the roasted peanuts and peanut butter. Prepare a batch the next time you plan a movie night, and serve them instead of popcorn or peanuts.

INGREDIENTS

Makes 12 cupcakes

Non-stick cooking spray

1 stick (4 ounces) unsalted butter, softened

⅓ cup smooth peanut butter

1 cup light brown sugar

3 large eggs

3 cups all-purpose flour

1 cup cornmeal

1 tablespoon baking powder

1 cup whole milk

⅓ cup roasted, unsalted peanuts, crushed

PREPARATION

1. Preheat oven to 375°F and line a standard cupcake pan with paper liners.

2. In the bowl of an electric mixer, cream butter, peanut butter, and sugar until smooth and airy. Add eggs, one at a time, beating well after each addition.

3. In a separate bowl, sift together flour, cornmeal, and baking powder.

4. Add flour mixture to butter mixture, alternating with milk, and beating on very low speed until just combined.

5. Fold in peanuts with as few strokes as possible.

6. Spoon batter into cupcake cups, filling each cup about three-quarters full.

7. Bake for about 20 minutes, or until a toothpick inserted in the center comes out clean.

8. Transfer pan to a wire rack and let cupcakes cool to room temperature.

9. Frost as desired and serve immediately, or store in an airtight container and refrigerate for up to 2 days.

Cinnamon Heart Cupcakes

If you love somebody who loves cupcakes, they will definitely love these. They're perfect for Valentine's Day, or any day you simply want to say "I love you!"

INGREDIENTS

Makes 12 cupcakes

Custard Filling (page 19)

Devil's Food Cupcakes (page 8)

Chocolate Buttercream Frosting (page 12)

¼ cup candy heart decorations

PREPARATION

1. Prepare filling, and refrigerate until ready to use.

2. Prepare cupcakes and cool completely.

3. Transfer chilled filling to a piping bag fitted with a round tip or to a squeeze bottle.

4. Insert tip into center of each cupcake and pipe in about 1 tablespoon of filling.

5. Prepare frosting, and spread on cupcake tops using a palette or flat knife.

6. If you like, pipe a bit of frosting into the center, too.

7. Decorate with candy hearts and serve.

Easter Egg and Bunny Cupcakes

Looking for an alternative to traditional Easter treats? These cute cupcakes can be topped with edible decorations such as sugar bunnies or eggs, or traditional chocolate eggs.

INGREDIENTS

Makes 12 cupcakes

Custard Filling (page 19)

Golden Sour Cream Cupcakes (page 9)

Buttercream Frosting (page 12)

Green gel food coloring

12 edible Easter decorations (such as bunnies, chocolate, or eggs)

PREPARATION

1. Prepare filling and refrigerate until ready to use.

2. Prepare cupcakes and cool completely.

3. Transfer chilled filling to a piping bag fitted with a round tip or to a squeeze bottle.

4. Insert tip into center of each cupcake and pipe in about 1 tablespoon of filling.

5. Prepare frosting, tint as desired, and transfer to a piping bag with a star tip.

6. Pipe frosting on cupcake tops; then place Easter decorations on top.

7. Serve immediately.

Fourth of July Cupcakes

Enjoy the 4th of July with your kids by preparing (and eating!) these cupcakes together. For a spectacular effect befitting the holiday, light a sparkler in each before serving.

INGREDIENTS

Makes 12 cupcakes

Vanilla Chocolate Chip Cupcakes (page 11)

Chocolate Buttercream Frosting (page 12)

Red, white, and blue edible glitter

12 sparklers

PREPARATION

1. Prepare cupcakes and cool completely.

2. Prepare frosting and spread generously on cupcake tops using a palate or flat knife.

3. Sprinkle cupcakes with glitter. Insert a sparkler into each cupcake, and light it just before serving.

Fresh Pumpkin Cupcakes

The grated, fresh pumpkin in these cupcakes gives them a light and moist texture. A refreshing, healthy change from canned pumpkin, and a great alternative to pumpkin pie.

INGREDIENTS

Makes 12 cupcakes

1 cup sugar

¾ cup canola oil

2 large eggs

1⅓ cups all-purpose flour

½ teaspoon baking powder

¼ teaspoon baking soda

1 teaspoon ground cinnamon

¼ teaspoon ground ginger

¼ teaspoon grated nutmeg

11 ounces pumpkin, peeled, seeded and grated

PREPARATION

1. Preheat oven to 350°F and line a standard cupcake pan with paper liners.

2. In the bowl of an electric mixer, mix sugar and oil for a few minutes. Add eggs, one at a time, beating well after each addition.

3. In a separate bowl, sift together flour, baking powder, baking soda, cinnamon, ginger, and nutmeg.

4. Fold flour mixture into oil mixture until just blended. Take care not to over mix. Gently fold in pumpkin.

5. Spoon batter into cupcake cups, filling each cup about three-quarters full. Bake for about 20 minutes, or until a toothpick inserted in the center comes out dry but with crumbs on it.

6. Transfer pan to a wire rack and cool cupcakes to room temperature.

7. Frost as desired and serve immediately, or store in an airtight container and refrigerate for up to 2 days.

Sweet and Scary Cupcakes

For a new twist on traditional treats, serve these decorated cupcakes at your next Halloween party. If you're expecting more than a dozen ghosts and goblins, make a double batch.

INGREDIENTS

Makes 12 cupcakes

Fresh Pumpkin Cupcakes (page 69)

Cream Cheese Frosting (page 13)

12 edible Halloween decorations (such as pumpkins, ghosts, and bats)

Orange edible glitter

PREPARATION

1. Prepare cupcakes and cool.

2. Prepare frosting and spread generously on cupcake tops using a palette or flat knife.

3. Place a Halloween decoration on each cupcake, sprinkle with glitter, and serve.

Spooky Spider Web Cupcakes

I recommend using parchment paper wrapped into a cone shape rather than a piping bag to pipe the chocolate glaze (see page 141). That way, you can reheat the chocolate in the microwave if needed.

INGREDIENTS

Makes 12 cupcakes

Fresh Pumpkin Cupcakes (page 69)

Chocolate Ganache Glaze (page 18)

6 ounces white chocolate, chopped into small pieces

PREPARATION

1. Prepare cupcakes and cool completely.

2. Prepare glaze and keep warm, shiny, and runny.

3. In the top of a double boiler, melt white chocolate until runny but still shiny. Transfer to a piping bag fitted with a #3 round tip or to a parchment triangle rolled for piping.

4. Decorate each cupcake completely before moving on to the next. First, drizzle on the warm glaze. While the glaze is still warm, pipe a small circle of white chocolate in the center. Make a slightly larger circle around this circle, then a third circle near the edge.

5. Before the glaze and white chocolate set, draw a toothpick from the middle of the cupcake towards the edge, carrying a ripple of melted chocolate and warm glaze along with it.

6. Repeat 5 more times to make 6 equally spaced lines extending from the center to the edge to form a web shape. If the white chocolate begins to solidify in the piping bag, heat it gently until runny again.

7. Refrigerate until glaze sets and serve.

Thanksgiving Cupcakes

Topped with friendly sugar decorations, these cupcakes are fun to serve and easy to make. If you're not crazy about pumpkin, use Gingerbread Cupcakes (page 34) instead.

INGREDIENTS

Makes 12 cupcakes

Fresh Pumpkin Cupcakes (page 69)

Chocolate Cream Cheese Frosting (page 13)

Orange edible glitter

12 edible Thanksgiving decorations (such as pumpkins or turkeys)

PREPARATION

1. Prepare cupcakes and cool completely.

2. Prepare frosting, and spread on cupcake tops using a palate or flat knife.

3. Top each cupcake with a pumpkin decoration, sprinkle with glitter, and serve.

Cupcakes For Kids

Love, Love, Love Cupcakes

•

Ice Cream Cone Cupcakes

•

Birthday Cake Cupcakes

•

Peanut Butter and Jelly Cupcakes

•

Sweet 16 Cupcakes

•

Rainbow Marshmallow Cupcakes

•

Pastel Party Cupcakes

•

Dotted Dalmatian Cupcakes

•

Boston Cream Cupcakes

•

Sweet Stenciled Cupcakes

•

Xs and Os

•

Chocolate Cups with Strawberry Chantilly Cream

Love, Love, Love Cupcakes

Show your kids you love them with hugs, kisses, and these heart-topped cupcakes. Serve them at your child's next birthday party, and people will be convinced you went to a professional bake shop.

INGREDIENTS

Makes 12 cupcakes

Golden Sour Cream Cupcakes (page 9)

Confectioner's sugar, for dusting

6 ounce red rolled fondants

6 ounces orange rolled fondant

¼ cup jam

PREPARATION

1. Prepare cupcakes and cool completely.

2. Dust work surface with confectioner's sugar. Roll out rolled fondant until it is about ⅛-inch thick. Use a 2¾-inch round cutter to cut out 6 red discs. Then use a small heart cutter to cut 4 hearts from each disc.

3. Reserve the removed hearts. Repeat with the orange rolled fondant.

4. Spread jam on cupcake tops, and lay a fondant disc on top of each cupcake.

5. Place contrasting color fondant hearts inside the heart-shaped spaces in every disc.

6. Serve immediately.

Ice Cream Cone Cupcakes

These soft-serve style ice cream cone cupcakes are made by inverting baked cupcakes on top of flat-bottomed ice cream cones.

INGREDIENTS

Makes 12 cupcakes

Vanilla Chocolate Chip Cupcakes (page 11)

Seven-Minute Frosting:
2 large egg whites

1½ cups sugar

5 tablespoons water

1½ teaspoons light corn syrup

¼ teaspoon cream of tartar

1 teaspoon pure vanilla extract or other extract flavor of choice

1 cup chocolate lentils, or candy of your choice

12 flat-bottomed ice-cream cones

½ cup blue and white jimmies

PREPARATION

1. Prepare cupcakes and cool completely.

2. Prepare frosting: Place egg whites, sugar, water, corn syrup, and cream of tartar in a heatproof bowl. Place bowl on a pot with about 2 inches of simmering water, and place pot on low heat. Make sure bottom of bowl does not come in contact with the water.

3. Whisk mixture vigorously using an electric hand mixer until soft peaks form and mixture reaches a temperature of 160°F on a candy thermometer. This will take about 7 minutes. Remove bowl from heat. Transfer mixture to bowl of an electric mixer, or use a hand blender fitted with a whisk attachment, and whisk for about 5 minutes, until stiff peaks form. Whisk in vanilla.

4. Carefully remove paper liners from cupcakes, and use a palette or flat knife to spread a bit of frosting on top.

5. Pour candy in bottom of each ice cream cone; then place inverted cupcakes on top so that frosted side touches the top of cone.

6. Transfer remaining frosting to a piping bag fitted with a star pastry tip and frost cupcake all around, so that it resembles a scoop of soft-serve ice cream.

7. Sprinkle with jimmies and serve.

Birthday Cake Cupcakes

Stack these cupcakes in a tower to make a playful, easy-to-serve "birthday cake." It's an ideal design for picnics and barbecues since there's no need for knives, plates, or forks.

INGREDIENTS

Makes 12 cupcakes

Triple Chocolate Cupcakes (page 10)

Chocolate Ganache Glaze (page 18)

⅓ cup rainbow jimmies

PREPARATION

1. Bake cupcakes and cool completely.

2. Prepare glaze. Top each cupcake with a teaspoon of glaze and sprinkle with jimmies.

3. Refrigerate until glaze sets.

4. Pile cupcakes in a tower on a serving dish, insert birthday candles, and serve.

Peanut Butter and Jelly Cupcakes

It's only natural that one of the world's most popular sandwiches makes a delicious cupcake, too. To make these a bit more decadent, top with Chocolate Buttercream Frosting (page 12), Peanut Butter Frosting (page 62), or slices of fresh bananas.

INGREDIENTS

Makes 12 cupcakes

½ stick (2 ounces) unsalted butter, softened

½ cup smooth peanut butter

⅔ cup light brown sugar

1 large egg

1¼ cups all-purpose flour

1½ teaspoons baking powder

Pinch of salt

⅔ cup whole milk

1 cup grape jelly

PREPARATION

1. Preheat oven to 350°F and line a standard cupcake pan with paper liners.

2. In the bowl of an electric mixer, cream butter, peanut butter, and sugar until creamy and airy. Beat in egg until fully blended.

3. In a separate bowl, sift together flour, baking powder, and salt.

4. Add flour mixture to butter mixture gradually, alternating with milk, and beating on very low speed just until batter forms. Take care not to over mix.

5. Spoon batter into cupcake cups, filling each cup about two-thirds full. Bake for about 20 minutes, or until a toothpick inserted in the center comes out clean. Transfer pan to a wire rack and let cupcakes cool to room temperature.

6. Scoop jelly into a piping bag fitted with a round tip or into a squeeze bottle. Insert tip into center of each cupcake and pipe in about 1 tablespoon jelly. Serve immediately.

Sweet 16 Cupcakes

Even when your Little Princess grows up, she'll be delighted to see these pretty cupcakes made especially in her honor.

INGREDIENTS

Makes 12 cupcakes

Golden Sour Cream Cupcakes (page 9)

Custard Filling (page 19)

Buttercream Frosting (page 12)

Pink gel food coloring

Pink edible glitter

PREPARATION

1. Prepare filling and refrigerate until ready to use.

2. Prepare cupcakes and cool completely.

3. Transfer chilled filling to a piping bag fitted with a round tip or to a squeeze bottle.

4. Insert tip into center of each cupcake and pipe in about 1 tablespoon of filling.

5. Prepare frosting, and tint with pink food coloring. Transfer icing to a piping bag fitted with a star pastry tip, and pipe a rose shape on top of each cupcake.

6. Sprinkle with glitter and serve.

Rainbow Marshmallow Cupcakes

Make sure you have extra marshmallows on hand to prevent the marshmallow-lovers in your house from eating the toppings before the cupcakes are served!

INGREDIENTS

Makes 12 cupcakes

Golden Sour Cream Cupcakes (page 9)

Buttercream Frosting (page 12)

12 large rainbow marshmallows

PREPARATION

1. Prepare cupcakes and cool completely.

2. Prepare frosting, and transfer to a piping bag fitted with a star decorating tip

3. Pipe frosting onto cupcakes and place a marshmallow on top.

4. Serve immediately.

Pastel Party Cupcakes

Though these cupcakes are perfect for birthday parties or baby showers, you don't need to wait for a special occasion. Serve them to cap off a Sunday supper or brighten up a rainy afternoon. Or hold a Cupcake Party, just for the fun of it!

INGREDIENTS

Makes 12 cupcakes

Vanilla Chocolate Chip Cupcakes (page 11)

Buttercream Frosting (page 12)

Pink, purple, green, and blue pastel gel food coloring

2 tablespoons pastel sugar sprinkles

PREPARATION

1. Prepare cupcakes and cool completely.

2. Prepare frosting, and divide into 4 bowls. Tint each bowl with a different color gel food coloring.

3. Spread frosting on cupcakes tops using a palette or flat knife, and decorate with sugar sprinkles.

4. Serve immediately.

Dotted Dalmatian Cupcakes

With coconut extract, coconut milk, and shredded coconut, these cupcakes are brimming in coco-nuttiness. They're delicious even without the sometimes hard-to-find coconut extract.

INGREDIENTS

Makes 24 cupcakes

1½ sticks (6 ounces) unsalted butter, softened

1½ cups sugar

1 teaspoon coconut extract

3 large eggs

2¼ cups all-purpose flour

1 teaspoon baking powder

½ teaspoon salt

1 cup coconut milk

⅓ cup unsweetened shredded coconut

1½ cups semi-sweet chocolate chips

PREPARATION

1. Preheat oven to 350°F and line a standard cupcake pan with paper liners.

2. In the bowl of an electric mixer, cream butter and sugar until fluffy and smooth. Add coconut extract; then add eggs, one at a time, beating well after each addition.

3. In a separate bowl, sift together flour, baking powder, and salt.

4. Add flour mixture to butter mixture gradually, alternating with coconut milk, and beating on very low speed just until batter forms. Take care not to over mix. Gently fold in shredded coconut and chocolate chips until evenly distributed.

5. Spoon batter into cupcake cups, filling each cup about two-thirds full. Bake for about 20 minutes, or until a toothpick inserted in the center comes out clean. Transfer pan to a wire rack and let cupcakes cool to room temperature.

6. Frost as desired and serve immediately, or store in an airtight container and refrigerate for up to 2 days.

Boston Cream Cupcakes

These cupcakes are inspired by one of my favorite cream-filled cakes. Golden cupcakes filled with homemade custard and topped with chocolate ganache glaze—what could be better?

INGREDIENTS

Makes 12 cupcakes

Custard Filling (page 19)

Golden Sour Cream Cupcakes (page 9)

Chocolate Ganache Glaze (page 18)

PREPARATION

1. Prepare filling and refrigerate until ready to use.

2. Prepare cupcakes and cool completely.

3. Transfer chilled filling to a piping bag fitted with a round tip or to a squeeze bottle.

4. Insert tip into center of each cupcake and pipe in about 1 tablespoon of filling.

5. Prepare glaze. Top each cupcake with 1 tablespoon glaze, refrigerate until glaze sets, and serve.

Sweet Stenciled Cupcakes

With rolled fondant, edible glitter, and stencils, every cupcake top is transformed into an artist's canvas. Select stencils and glitter colors that suit your occasion. The recommendations here are perfect to welcome the spring or celebrate a baby shower or first birthday.

INGREDIENTS

Makes 12 cupcakes

Golden Sour Cream Cupcakes (page 9)

Confectioner's sugar, for dusting

15 ounces white rolled fondant

¼ cup jam

Water, for brushing

Green, pink, yellow, and red edible glitter

PREPARATION

1. Prepare cupcakes and cool completely.

2. Dust work surface with confectioner's sugar; then roll out rolled fondant until it is about ⅛-inch thick. Use a 2¾-inch round cutter to cut out 12 discs.

3. Spread cupcake tops with jam and lay fondant discs on top.

4. Place stencil on each disc and brush exposed areas with a bit of water.

5. Sprinkle on glitter and carefully remove stencil.

6. Serve immediately.

Xs and Os

Everyone wins with this design. Decorate the cupcakes with your favorite colors of chocolate lentils, and select frosting colors to match. Arrange nine of the cupcakes in an X and O pattern (set aside the additional three cupcakes for second helpings!)

INGREDIENTS

Makes 12 cupcakes

Vanilla Chocolate Chip Cupcakes (page 11)

Buttercream Frosting (page 12)

Green and blue gel food coloring

1¼ cups green and blue chocolate lentils

PREPARATION

1. Prepare cupcakes and cool completely.

2. Prepare frosting, and divide evenly between two bowls.

3. Tint one bowl with blue coloring and the other with green coloring.

4. Frost 6 cupcakes with green frosting, and top with blue lentils arranged in an O shape.

5. Frost the remaining 6 cupcakes with blue frosting, and top with green lentils arranged in an X shape.

6. Serve immediately.

Chocolate Cups with Strawberry Chantilly Cream

These elegant cupcakes combine readymade chocolate cups with homemade vanilla-scented whipped cream and chopped strawberries. If you use a vanilla bean, grind the leftover pod and add it to your sugar container to make vanilla-scented sugar. For best results when making Chantilly cream, make sure that both the whipping cream and mixing bowl are chilled thoroughly before mixing.

INGREDIENTS

Makes 4 cups

10 to 15 large strawberries

1 vanilla bean, split lengthwise, or 1 teaspoon natural vanilla extract

1 cup heavy (whipping) cream, thoroughly chilled

3 tablespoons confectioner's sugar

Four ½-cup chocolate dessert cups

PREPARATION

1. Put the bowl of your electric mixer in the freezer to chill. In the meantime, wash strawberries thoroughly, pat dry, and remove stems.

2. Slice 1 strawberry vertically into thin slices and set aside. Chop remaining strawberries into small pieces.

3. Scrape vanilla seeds from pod. Place cream, sugar, and vanilla seeds in chilled mixing bowl and whip on medium speed until soft peaks form.

4. Gently fold in chopped strawberries until combined.

5. Transfer cream to a piping bag fitted with a star pastry tip, and pipe into chocolate dessert cups.

6. Garnish each cup with a slice of strawberry, and serve immediately.

Sweet and Special Muffins

Apple, Pear, and Spice Muffins

•

Banana Walnut Muffins

•

Carrot, Pumpkin, and Raisin Muffins

•

Wine-Marinated Pear Muffins with Almond Streusel

•

Very Berry Muffins

•

Orange, Ricotta, and Honey Muffins

•

Lemon Poppy Seed Muffins

Apple, Pear, and Spice Muffins

Serve these muffins with a cup of hot tea as a perfect autumn breakfast or tea-time snack. The recipe contains a mixture of spices; adjust them according to your preference, and savor the flavor.

INGREDIENTS

Makes 12 small muffins

Non-stick cooking spray

2 large eggs

6 tablespoons sugar

¾ cup whole milk

1 stick (4 ounces) unsalted butter, melted and cooled to room temperature

2¼ cups all-purpose flour

1 tablespoon plus 1 teaspoon baking powder

¼ teaspoon salt

1 teaspoon ground cinnamon

½ teaspoon ground ginger

¼ teaspoon ground nutmeg

¼ to ⅛ teaspoon ground cloves

⅛ teaspoon ground cardamom

2 Golden Delicious apples, peeled, cored, cut into very small cubes

2 Anjou or Bartlett pears, peeled, cored, and cut into very small cubes

12 round slices of a cored but unpeeled apple

Unsalted butter, melted, for brushing

PREPARATION

1. Preheat oven to 375°F. Line a cupcake pan with paper liners, or grease with non-stick cooking spray.

2. In a large bowl, mix together eggs and sugar. Mix in milk until blended; then add butter, mixing until well combined.

3. In a separate bowl, sift together flour, baking powder, salt, cinnamon, ginger, nutmeg, cloves, and cardamom.

4. Gently fold flour mixture into butter mixture until just blended. Take care not to over mix. Fold in apples and pears in as few strokes as possible.

5. Spoon batter into muffin cups, filling each cup about three-quarters full. Top each muffin with a slice of apple and brush with butter. Bake for about 20 minutes, or until a toothpick inserted in the center comes out dry. Transfer pan to a wire rack and let muffins cool for about 15 minutes. Serve warm.

Banana Walnut Muffins

The lovely banana taste and aroma of these muffins are a perfect accompaniment to a fresh cup of coffee. If you like, replace the cinnamon with 1 teaspoon pure vanilla extract, and add it with the bananas.

INGREDIENTS

Makes 6 muffins

Non-stick cooking spray

2 large eggs

¾ stick (3 ounces) unsalted butter, melted and cooled to room temperature

3 large very ripe bananas, mashed

¼ cup buttermilk

1 teaspoon ground cinnamon

⅔ cup light brown sugar

2 cups all-purpose flour

¾ teaspoon baking soda

Pinch of salt

1 cup toasted walnuts

PREPARATION

1. Preheat oven to 350°F. Line a standard muffin pan with paper liners, or grease with non-stick cooking spray.

2. In a large bowl, lightly whisk eggs, butter, bananas, and buttermilk until combined.

3. In a separate bowl, sift together cinnamon, brown sugar, flour, baking soda, and salt. Mix in walnuts.

4. Fold flour mixture into banana mixture until just blended. Take care not to over mix.

5. Spoon batter into muffin cups, filling each cup about three-quarters full.

6. Bake for about 20 minutes, or until a toothpick inserted in the center comes out clean.

7. Transfer pan to a wire rack and let muffins cool for about 15 minutes.

8. Serve warm.

Carrot, Pumpkin, and Raisin Muffins

Sweet and spicy, moist and satisfying, these muffins go very well with your morning coffee. Serve them with yogurt or cottage cheese for a delicious midday snack.

INGREDIENTS

Makes 6 muffins

Non-stick cooking spray

¾ cup light brown sugar

¼ cup honey

¾ cup canola oil

2 large eggs

1⅓ cups all-purpose flour

½ teaspoon baking powder

¼ teaspoon baking soda

1 teaspoon ground cinnamon

¼ teaspoon ground ginger

¼ teaspoon grated nutmeg

6 ounces (about 1¼ cups) grated carrots

5 ounces peeled, seeded, and grated pumpkin

3 tablespoons raisins

PREPARATION

1. Preheat oven to 350°F. Line a standard muffin pan with paper liners, or grease with non-stick cooking spray.

2. In the bowl of an electric mixer, beat sugar, honey, and oil until combined. Add eggs, one at a time, beating well after each addition.

3. In a separate bowl, sift together flour, baking powder, baking soda, cinnamon, ginger, and nutmeg.

4. Add flour mixture to egg mixture while mixing slowly, until just blended. Take care not to over mix. Fold in carrots, pumpkin, and raisins with as few strokes as possible.

5. Spoon batter into muffin cups, filling each cup about three-quarters full.

6. Bake for about 20 minutes, or until a toothpick inserted in the center comes out dry but with crumbs on it.

7. Transfer pan to a wire rack and let muffins cool for about 15 minutes.

8. Serve warm.

Wine-Marinated Pear Muffins with Almond Streusel

Elaborate yet comforting, this dessert takes a bit of advance preparation, but the result is worth it. Start marinating the pears two or three days in advance to give them plenty of time to absorb the wine syrup. You can also make the streusel in advance and store it in the refrigerator or freezer. Make sure the butter for the streusel is cold, and mix only until crumbs form.

INGREDIENTS

Makes 6 muffins

Pears:

3 cups dry red wine

1 cup sugar

1 cinnamon stick

¼ teaspoon finely grated orange zest (from ¼ orange)

1 clove

6 Anjou or Bartlett pears, peeled, cored, and quartered

Water, to cover

PREPARATION

1. Prepare pears: In a medium saucepan, combine wine, sugar, cinnamon, orange zest, and clove, and bring to a boil over medium-high heat.

2. Add pears and stir, making sure they are completely covered in wine syrup. Add water, if necessary, until pears are covered.

3. Reduce heat to low, and simmer for 20 minutes, until pears are tender but still hold their shape.

4. Remove from heat and cool to room temperature. Transfer pears and syrup to a plastic container, close securely, and refrigerate for up to 3 days to allow pears to marinate.

5. Prepare muffins: Preheat oven to 375°F. Line a standard muffin pan with paper liners, or grease with non-stick cooking spray.

(continued on next page)

(continued from previous page)

Muffins:

Non-stick cooking spray

2 large eggs

¾ cup whole milk

1 stick (4 ounces) unsalted butter, melted and cooled to room temperature

1 cup light brown sugar

2¾ cups all-purpose flour

1 tablespoon baking powder

1 teaspoon ground cinnamon

¼ teaspoon salt

Almond Streusel:

5 tablespoons ground almonds

4 tablespoons confectioner's sugar

2 tablespoons light brown sugar

5½ ounces all-purpose flour

1 teaspoon pure vanilla extract or ground cinnamon

1 stick (4 ounces) unsalted butter, very cold, cut into small pieces

6. Drain pears and reserve syrup for sauce. Cut pears into small cubes and set aside.

7. In a large bowl, whisk together egg, milk, butter, and sugar until combined.

8. In a separate bowl, sift together flour, baking powder, cinnamon, and salt.

9. Gently fold flour mixture into butter mixture until just blended. Take care not to over mix.

10. Fold in pear cubes in as few strokes as possible.

11. Prepare streusel: In the bowl of an electric mixer, place almonds, sugars, flour, vanilla, and butter. Mix on low speed just until crumbs form.

12. Spoon batter into muffin cups, filling each cup about two-thirds full.

13. Sprinkle with streusel; then bake for 15 to 20 minutes, or until a toothpick inserted in the center comes out dry.

14. Transfer pan to a wire rack and let muffins cool for about 15 minutes.

15. Serve warm, with the reserved syrup.

Very Berry Muffins

You can enjoy these muffins all year long since they are excellent with either frozen or fresh berries. Add frozen berries to the batter while they are still frozen, to keep their color from running.

INGREDIENTS

Makes 12 small muffins

Non-stick cooking spray

2 large eggs

1 cup whole milk

$\frac{7}{8}$ stick (3$\frac{1}{2}$ ounces) unsalted butter, melted and cooled to room temperature

1 teaspoon pure vanilla extract

$\frac{1}{2}$ cup sugar

2 cups plus 2 tablespoons all-purpose flour

1 tablespoon baking powder

$\frac{1}{2}$ teaspoon salt

$\frac{1}{4}$ teaspoon grated lemon zest (from 1 lemon)

7 ounces mixed berries, fresh or frozen and separated into individual berries

PREPARATION

1. Preheat oven to 375°F. Line a standard cupcake pan with paper liners, or grease with non-stick cooking spray.

2. In a large bowl, lightly whisk eggs, milk, butter, vanilla, and sugar until combined.

3. In a separate bowl, sift together flour, baking powder, salt, and lemon zest.

4. Gently fold flour mixture into butter mixture until just blended. Take care not to over mix.

5. Fold in berries with as few strokes as possible until evenly distributed.

6. Spoon batter into muffin cups, filling each cup about three-quarters full.

7. Bake for about 20 minutes, or until a toothpick inserted in the center comes out dry.

8. Transfer pan to a wire rack and let muffins cool for about 15 minutes.

9. Serve warm.

Orange, Ricotta, and Honey Muffins

These muffins feature the delicious trio of orange, ricotta cheese, and honey. Serve them warm, topped with butter and honey, for a truly divine breakfast.

INGREDIENTS

Makes 12 muffins

Non-stick cooking spray

1 large egg

¼ cup honey

¾ cup orange juice

¼ cup (1 ounce) unsalted butter, melted and cooled to room temperature

2 tablespoons whole milk

2 cups all-purpose flour

2 teaspoons baking powder

½ teaspoon baking soda

¼ teaspoon salt

1 tablespoon finely grated orange zest (from 2 oranges)

¾ cup unsalted ricotta cheese

PREPARATION

1. Preheat oven to 400°F. Line a standard cupcake pan with paper liners, or grease with non-stick cooking spray.

2. In a medium bowl, lightly whisk egg, honey, orange juice, butter, and milk until combined.

3. In a separate bowl, combine flour, baking powder, baking soda, salt, and orange zest until combined.

4. Gently fold flour mixture into butter mixture until just blended.

5. Spoon two-thirds of the batter into muffin cups, filling each cup about one-half full.

6. Distribute ricotta evenly among the muffin cups; then top with remaining batter.

7. Make sure a bit of ricotta is visible on the top.

8. Bake for about 20 minutes, or until a toothpick inserted in the center comes out dry.

9. Transfer pan to a wire rack and let muffins cool for about 15 minutes.

10. Serve warm.

Lemon Poppy Seed Muffins

Citrus rinds are an excellent natural extract. They contribute so much flavor to this recipe that there's no need for lemon juice. For a tangy alternative, replace 1 tablespoon of the lemon zest with lime zest.

INGREDIENTS

Makes 8 muffins

Non-stick cooking spray

2 large eggs

1 cup whole milk

6½ tablespoons canola oil

6 tablespoons sugar

2¾ cups all-purpose flour

3 teaspoons baking powder

¼ teaspoon salt

4 tablespoons poppy seeds

2 tablespoons finely grated lemon zest (from 4 lemons)

Royal Icing (page 14)

PREPARATION

1. Preheat oven to 400°F. Line a standard muffin pan with paper liners, or grease with non-stick cooking spray.

2. In a medium bowl, lightly whisk eggs, milk, and oil until combined. Mix in sugar.

3. In a separate bowl, sift together flour, baking powder, and salt. Mix in poppy seeds.

4. Gently fold flour mixture and lemon zest into egg mixture until just blended.

5. Spoon batter into muffin cups, filling each cup about three-quarters full.

6. Bake for about 20 minutes, or until a toothpick inserted in the center comes out dry.

7. Transfer pan to a wire rack and let muffins cool for about 15 minutes.

8. Serve warm.

Health Conscious Muffins

Dairy-Free Carrot Apple Muffins

•

Banana, Date, and Walnut Bran Muffins

•

Bran Muffin Breakfast Bowls

•

Egg-Free Double Chocolate Muffins

•

Zucchini, Carrot, and Pistachio Muffins

•

Oatmeal, Yogurt, and Cinnamon Muffins

Dairy-Free Carrot Apple Muffins

This recipe, which uses oil rather than butter and whole-wheat flour rather than white, will appeal to people who shun dairy products or refined flour.

INGREDIENTS

Makes 6 muffins

Non-stick cooking spray

2 large eggs

½ cup canola oil

½ cup date honey or honey

1½ cups whole-wheat flour

2 teaspoons baking powder

1 teaspoon baking soda

1 teaspoon ground cinnamon

1½ cups finely grated carrots

2 tart apples, peeled, cored, and coarsely grated

½ cup chopped walnuts

PREPARATION

1. Preheat oven to 375°F. Line a standard muffin pan with paper liners, or grease with non-stick cooking spray.

2. In a mixing bowl, lightly whisk eggs, oil, and date honey until combined.

3. In a separate bowl, sift together flour, baking powder, baking soda, and cinnamon.

4. Fold flour mixture into egg mixture until just blended. Take care not to over mix. Fold in carrots, apples, and walnuts with as few strokes as possible.

5. Spoon batter into muffin cups, filling each cup about three-quarters full

6. Bake for about 20 minutes, or until a toothpick inserted in the center comes out dry.

7. Transfer pan to a wire rack and let muffins cool for about 15 minutes.

8. Serve warm.

Banana, Date, and Walnut Bran Muffins

These muffins are particularly delicious with fresh dates and date honey, but if you can't find those at your supermarket, dried dates and regular honey are just fine. If you use fresh dates, remove the peel before chopping them.

INGREDIENTS

Makes 18 muffins

Non-stick cooking spray

1½ sticks (6 ounces) unsalted butter, softened

⅓ cup light brown sugar

⅓ cup date honey or honey

4 medium very ripe bananas, mashed

3 large eggs

2 cups all-purpose flour

½ teaspoon salt

1½ tablespoons baking soda

1½ cups bran

1 cup chopped walnuts

10 large fresh dates, peeled, pitted, and chopped

PREPARATION

1. Preheat oven to 375°F. Line a standard muffin pan with paper liners, or grease with non-stick cooking spray.

2. In the bowl of an electric mixer, cream butter and sugar until fluffy and smooth. Add date honey and bananas and mix until combined. Add eggs, one at a time, beating well after each addition.

3. In a separate bowl, sift together flour, salt, and baking soda. Mix in bran, walnuts, and dates.

4. Add flour mixture to banana mixture while mixing slowly, until just blended.

5. Spoon batter into muffin cups, filling each cup about three-quarters full.

6. Bake for about 20 minutes, or until a toothpick inserted in the center comes out dry.

7. Transfer pan to a wire rack and let muffins cool for about 15 minutes.

8. Serve warm.

Bran Muffin Breakfast Bowls

Give your morning an innovative start by using fresh bran muffins as a serving bowl for yogurt and fresh fruit salad. Drizzle with honey for a delicious, wholesome, and attractive breakfast.

INGREDIENTS

Makes 12 muffins

Non-stick cooking spray

1½ cups bran

⅓ cup boiling water

1 stick (4 ounces) unsalted butter, softened

1 cup light brown sugar

2 tablespoons molasses

2 large eggs

1¼ cups whole-wheat flour

¾ cup all-purpose flour

2 teaspoons baking soda

1 teaspoon baking powder

PREPARATION

1. Preheat oven to 375°F and grease a standard muffin pan with non-stick cooking spray.

2. In a heatproof bowl, mix together bran and boiling water. Set aside to cool to room temperature.

3. In the bowl of an electric mixer, cream butter and sugar until fluffy and smooth.

4. Mix in molasses; then add eggs, one at a time, beating well after each addition.

5. Beat bran mixture into egg mixture until combined.

6. In a separate bowl, sift together flours, baking soda, baking powder, and cinnamon.

7. Add flour mixture to bran mixture slowly, alternating with buttermilk and milk, until just blended.

8. Spoon batter into muffins cups, filling each cup about two-thirds full.

(continued on next page)

(continued from previous page)

1 teaspoon ground cinnamon

1 cup buttermilk

¼ cup whole milk

Topping:

6 cups plain yogurt

¾ cup fresh fruit salad

Honey, for drizzling

9. Bake for about 20 minutes, or until a toothpick inserted in the center comes out dry.

10. Transfer pan to a wire rack and let muffins cool for about 15 minutes; then turn out muffins and cool completely.

11. With the muffins upright, use a serrated knife to hollow out the middle of each to make a bowl. Be sure to leave a ½-inch base at the bottom of the muffins.

12. Reserve removed muffin for another use (as a great base for cheesecake, for instance).

13. Spoon ½ cup yogurt into each muffin bowl, add 1 tablespoon fruit salad, and drizzle with honey

14. Serve immediately.

Egg-Free Double Chocolate Muffins

An allergy to eggs shouldn't prevent you from enjoying delicious chocolate muffins. With this recipe, you can make sure everyone gets to indulge in this super chocolaty treat.

INGREDIENTS

Makes 12 small muffins

Non-stick cooking spray

¼ cup canola oil

4 tablespoons plain yogurt

1 cup buttermilk

2 cups all-purpose flour

2 teaspoons baking powder

1 teaspoon baking soda

3 tablespoons unsweetened cocoa powder

¾ cup light brown sugar

1 cup white chocolate chips

PREPARATION

1. Preheat oven to 350°F. Line a standard muffin pan with paper liners, or grease with non-stick cooking spray.

2. In a medium bowl, mix together oil, yogurt, and buttermilk.

3. In a separate bowl, sift together flour, baking powder, baking soda, and cocoa powder. Mix in sugar.

4. Fold oil mixture into flour mixture until just blended. Take care not to over mix. Fold in chocolate chips with as few strokes as possible.

5. Spoon batter into muffin cups, filling each cup about three-quarters full.

6. Bake for 12 to 15 minutes, or until muffins are high and baked through.

7. Transfer pan to a wire rack and let muffins cool for about 15 minutes.

8. Serve warm.

Zucchini, Carrot, and Pistachio Muffins

These muffins are so delicious that no one will suspect you've hidden carrots and zucchini in them! Omit the pistachio nuts if you plan on serving these to young children.

INGREDIENTS

Makes 12 muffins

Non-stick cooking spray

1 cup canola oil

2 large eggs

1 cup light brown sugar

⅓ cup date honey or honey

2 cups grated zucchini

1 cup grated carrots

2 cups all-purpose flour

1 cup whole-wheat flour

2 teaspoons baking soda

2 teaspoons ground cinnamon

½ cup roughly chopped, unsalted pistachio nuts, plus more for topping

PREPARATION

1. Preheat oven to 375°F. Line a standard muffin pan with paper liners, or grease with non-stick cooking spray.

2. In the bowl of an electric mixer, combine oil, eggs, sugar, and honey. Add zucchini and carrots and mix until combined.

3. In a separate bowl, sift together flour, baking soda, and cinnamon. Mix in pistachios.

4. Fold flour mixture into egg mixture until just blended. Take care not to over mix.

5. Spoon batter into muffin cups, filling each cup about two-thirds full.

6. Sprinkle with pistachios; then bake for about 20 minutes, or until a toothpick inserted in the center comes out dry.

7. Transfer pan to a wire rack and let muffins cool for about 15 minutes.

8. Serve warm.

Oatmeal, Yogurt, and Cinnamon Muffins

These nourishing muffins contain oatmeal, yogurt, and whole-wheat flour. They are a great way to start your day with good taste and good health.

INGREDIENTS

Makes 6 muffins

Non-stick cooking spray

½ cup plain yogurt

½ cup whole milk

1 large egg

¼ cup vegetable oil

¼ cup light brown sugar

1 cup all-purpose flour

½ cup whole-wheat flour

1 cup quick-cooking oats

1 tablespoon baking powder

1 teaspoon ground cinnamon

Pinch of salt

Topping:
2 tablespoons light brown sugar

2 tablespoons quick-cooking oats

PREPARATION

1. Prepare muffins: Preheat oven to 375°F. Line a standard muffin pan with paper liners, or grease with non-stick cooking spray.

2. In a large bowl, mix together yogurt, milk, egg, and oil until combined. Mix in sugar.

3. In a separate bowl, combine flours, oats, baking powder, cinnamon, and salt until combined.

4. Fold flour mixture into yogurt mixture until just blended. Take care not to over mix.

5. Prepare topping: In a small bowl, combine sugar and oats.

6. Spoon batter into muffin cups, filling each cup about two-thirds full.

7. Sprinkle with topping; then bake for 12 to 15 minutes, or until a toothpick inserted in the center comes out dry.

8. Transfer pan to a wire rack and let muffins cool for about 15 minutes.

9. Serve warm.

Savory Muffins

Cream Cheese, Dill, and Cornmeal Muffins

•

Mexican-Style Cornmeal Muffins

•

Roasted Vegetable Muffins

•

Spinach, Ricotta, and Pine Nut Muffins

•

Pesto Muffins

•

Zucchini and Dill Muffins

•

Bacon, Olive, Cheese, and Thyme Muffins

Cream Cheese, Dill, and Cornmeal Muffins

Looking for an eye-catching way to serve smoked salmon at your next Sunday brunch? Try tucking it into these tasty muffins, with cream cheese and red onions.

INGREDIENTS

Makes 6 large muffins

Non-stick cooking spray

2 large eggs

1/3 cup cream cheese, plus more for serving

3 tablespoons unsalted butter, melted and cooled to room temperature

2/3 cup buttermilk

1/4 cup roughly chopped dill, plus more for serving

1 cup all-purpose flour

2 teaspoons baking powder

1/2 teaspoon baking soda

1/2 teaspoon salt

1 cup cornmeal

Cream cheese

Smoked salmon

Red onion

PREPARATION

1. Preheat oven to 400°F. Line a standard muffin pan with paper liners, or grease with non-stick cooking spray.

2. In a large bowl, lightly whisk eggs, cream cheese, butter, buttermilk, and dill until combined.

3. In a separate bowl, sift together flour, baking powder, baking soda, and salt. Mix in cornmeal.

4. Gently fold flour mixture into egg mixture until just blended. Take care not to over mix.

5. Spoon batter into muffin cups, filling each cup about three-quarters full.

6. Bake for 15 to 20 minutes, or until a toothpick inserted in the center comes out dry.

7. Transfer pan to a wire rack and let muffins cool completely.

8. To serve, slice muffins horizontally just below the top.

9. Spread bottom half with cream cheese, and top with smoked salmon, fresh dill, and onion.

10. Serve with capers and lemon wedges on the side.

Mexican-Style Cornmeal Muffins

No time to travel south for a holiday? So why not treat yourself to a batch of warm cornmeal muffins, served with fresh guacamole and salsa.

INGREDIENTS

Makes 14 small muffins

Non-stick cooking spray

1½ sticks (6 ounces) unsalted butter, melted and cooled to room temperature

2 large eggs

2 cups buttermilk

2 cups all-purpose flour

2 cups yellow cornmeal

⅔ cups sugar

1½ tablespoons baking powder

½ teaspoon salt

2½ cups guacamole, optional

2½ cups tomato salsa, optional

PREPARATION

1. Preheat oven to 375°F. Line a standard muffin pan with paper liners, or grease with non-stick cooking spray.

2. In a medium bowl, mix together butter, eggs, and buttermilk.

3. In a separate bowl, combine flour, cornmeal, sugar, baking powder, and salt.

4. Fold flour mixture into butter mixture until just blended. Take care not to over mix.

5. Spoon batter into muffin cups, filling each cup about three-quarters full.

6. Bake for about 25 minutes, or until a toothpick inserted in the center comes out dry.

7. Transfer pan to a wire rack and cool completely.

8. Serve with guacamole and salsa on the side.

Roasted Vegetable Muffins

Add these colorful muffins to your table for brunch or lunch, alongside an arugula and parmesan salad.

INGREDIENTS

Makes 12 muffins

Roasted vegetables:

1 cup assorted vegetables (zucchini, sweet potato, peppers, eggplant, mushrooms, leeks, pumpkin, broccoli, etc.), cut into small cubes

2 tablespoons extra-virgin olive oil

Salt, to taste

Freshly ground black pepper, to taste

Dried rosemary, thyme, or oregano, to taste

PREPARATION

1. Preheat oven to 400°F and line a baking sheet with parchment paper.

2. Prepare vegetables: Place vegetables in a medium bowl. Add oil, salt, pepper, and rosemary, and toss gently to coat.

3. Transfer to a baking sheet and roast for about 20 minutes, until vegetables are golden and ready to eat. Remove from oven and set aside.

4. Prepare muffins: Reduce heat to 375°F. Line a standard muffin pan with paper liners, or grease with non-stick cooking spray.

5. In a medium bowl, lightly whisk together butter, egg, and milk. Gently fold in mozzarella cheese until just combined.

(continued on next page)

(continued from previous page)

Muffins:

Non-stick cooking spray

¾ stick (3 ounces) unsalted butter, melted and cooled to room temperature

1 large egg

1 cup whole milk

1 cup coarsely grated mozzarella cheese

2¼ cups all-purpose flour

2½ teaspoons baking powder

1 teaspoon sugar

½ teaspoon salt

½ cup crumbled feta cheese

¼ cup pesto sauce

6. In a separate bowl, sift together flour, baking powder, sugar, and salt.

7. Fold flour mixture into egg mixture just until blended.

8. Spoon two-thirds of the batter into the muffin cups, filling each cup about one-third full.

9. Top with half the roasted vegetables and all the feta cheese and pesto.

10. Add remaining batter and vegetables.

11. Bake for about 20 minutes, or until a toothpick inserted in the center comes out dry.

12. Transfer pan to a wire rack and let muffins cool for about 15 minutes.

13. Serve warm.

Spinach, Ricotta, and Pine Nut Muffins

Mid-morning brunch, a lunchtime bowl of tomato soup, or evening cocktails are all excellent opportunities for serving these flavorful muffins. Add some chopped basil or coriander leaves for extra flavor.

INGREDIENTS

Makes 12 small muffins

Non-stick cooking spray

Salted water

9 ounces fresh spinach leaves

1 cup salted ricotta cheese

½ cup coarsely grated cheddar cheese

Pinch of ground nutmeg

3 tablespoons lightly toasted pine nuts

2 large eggs

½ cup whole milk

½ cup buttermilk

2 cups all-purpose flour

1 tablespoon baking powder

1 teaspoon salt

PREPARATION

1. Preheat oven to 375°F. Line a standard muffin pan with paper liners, or grease with non-stick cooking spray.

2. In a small pot, bring salted water to a boil. Add spinach leaves and blanch for about 30 seconds. Transfer spinach to a colander, and run under cold water to stop the cooking process. Drain spinach thoroughly; then transfer to a small bowl and mix with cheeses, nutmeg, and pine nuts. Set aside.

3. In a large bowl, lightly whisk eggs, milk, and buttermilk.

4. In a medium bowl, sift together flour, baking powder, and salt.

5. Fold flour mixture into egg mixture until just blended. Do not over mix. Fold in spinach mixture using as few strokes as possible.

6. Spoon batter into muffin cups, filling each cup about three-quarters full.

7. Bake for 12 to 15 minutes, or until a toothpick inserted in the center comes out dry.

8. Transfer pan to a wire rack and let muffins cool for about 15 minutes.

9. Serve warm.

Pesto Muffins

Pesto, the classic Italian condiment, gives these intriguing muffins a fresh, flavorful twist. With feta cheese and roasted pine nuts included right in the batter, they are a perfect complement to a fresh tomato salad.

INGREDIENTS

Makes 12 muffins

Non-stick cooking spray

1 large egg

1 cup whole milk

¾ stick (3 ounces) unsalted butter, melted and cooled to room temperature

1 cup coarsely grated cheddar cheese

2¼ cups all-purpose flour

2½ teaspoons baking powder

1 teaspoon sugar

½ teaspoon salt

¾ cup pesto

10 tablespoons crumbled feta cheese

⅓ cup toasted pine nuts

PREPARATION

1. Preheat oven to 375°F. Line a standard muffin pan with paper liners, or grease with non-stick cooking spray.

2. In a large bowl, lightly whisk egg, milk, and butter until combined. Gently fold in cheddar cheese until just blended.

3. In a separate bowl, sift together flour, baking powder, sugar, and salt.

4. Fold flour mixture into butter mixture until just blended.

5. Using as few strokes as possible, fold in pesto, feta cheese, and pine nuts. Take care not to over mix; the batter should be thick and chunky, not smooth.

6. Spoon batter into muffin cups, filling each cup about three-quarters full.

7. Bake for about 20 minutes, or until a toothpick inserted in the center comes out dry.

8. Transfer pan to a wire rack and let muffins cool for about 15 minutes.

9. Serve warm.

Zucchini and Dill Muffins

Inspired by Greek zucchini patties, these muffins are excellent alongside tzatziki, a fresh dip made with yogurt, garlic, lemon juice and dill. If you like, add a bit of fresh mint along with the dill.

INGREDIENTS

Makes 12 muffins

Non-stick cooking spray

1 large egg

1 cup whole milk

¾ stick (3 ounces) unsalted butter, melted and cooled to room temperature

1 cup grated zucchini

3 tablespoons roughly chopped fresh dill

2¼ cups all-purpose flour

2½ teaspoons baking powder

1 teaspoon sugar

½ teaspoon salt

1 cup coarsely grated cheddar cheese

½ cup crumbled feta cheese

PREPARATION

1. Preheat oven to 375°F. Line a standard muffin pan with paper liners, or grease with non-stick cooking spray.

2. In a large bowl, lightly whisk egg, milk, and butter until combined. Gently fold in zucchini and dill until just combined.

3. In a separate bowl, sift together flour, baking powder, sugar, and salt.

4. Fold flour mixture into egg mixture until just blended. Do not over mix.

5. Fold in cheeses with as few strokes as possible.

6. Spoon batter into muffin cups, filling each cup about three-quarters full.

7. Bake for about 20 minutes, or until a toothpick inserted in the center comes out dry.

8. Transfer pan to a wire rack and cool for about 15 minutes.

9. Serve warm.

Bacon, Olive, Cheese, and Thyme Muffins

This distinct muffin is a worthy accompaniment to scrambled eggs. Your satisfied guests may surprise you by asking for seconds.

INGREDIENTS

Makes 12 muffins

Non-stick cooking spray

3 ounces bacon, chopped

¾ stick (3 ounces) unsalted butter, melted and cooled to room temperature

1 large egg

1 cup whole milk

2¼ cups all-purpose flour

2½ teaspoons baking powder

1 teaspoon sugar

½ teaspoon salt

¼ cup pitted black olives, chopped

1 teaspoon fresh (or dried) thyme

1 cup coarsely grated cheddar cheese

PREPARATION

1. Preheat oven to 375°F. Line a standard muffin pan with paper liners, or grease with non-stick cooking spray.

2. In a frying pan over medium heat, or in a microwave, cook bacon until crispy and brown. Drain off fat and set aside.

3. In a medium bowl, whisk together butter, egg, and milk until combined.

4. In a separate bowl, sift together flour, baking powder, sugar, and salt.

5. Fold flour mixture into butter mixture until just blended. Take care not to over mix.

6. Using as few strokes as possible, fold in olives, thyme, cheese, and bacon.

7. Spoon batter into muffin cups, filling each cup about three-quarters full.

8. Bake for about 20 minutes, or until a toothpick inserted in the center comes out clean.

9. Transfer pan to a wire rack and let muffins cool for about 15 minutes.

10. Serve warm.

Tips, Tools, and Ingredients

TIPS

Mixing

Cupcake and muffin batter should never be over mixed. Once you add flour to the liquid ingredients, mix only until combined. Otherwise, the gluten in the flour will start developing, and the batter will become elastic. Don't worry if the batter seems a bit lumpy just before baking. The finished product will be just fine.

Serving and storing cupcakes

Cupcakes are best eaten fresh, on the day they're baked. If you want to bake them a day or two in advance, freeze them right after they cool and defrost them outside the refrigerator. Apply frosting when they reach room temperature and serve them soon afterward. To ensure that your cupcakes don't absorb freezer odors or get damaged by frost, wrap them individually in plastic cling wrap before storing them in a plastic container and freezing. Cupcakes that contain fresh vegetables such as carrot or pumpkin are quite moist, and they can generally be refrigerated for up to 3 days in an airtight container.

I recommend topping cupcakes with frosting. Not only do they look fabulous when topped with something fluffy, creamy, and sweet; the frosting also provides a lovely, moist contrast to the cake-like texture of the cupcake. Many of the cupcakes in this book include a filling, making the cupcake even more decadent.

Serving and storing muffins

Muffins are also best eaten fresh, on the day they're baked. They are most tasty when warm, so if they've already cooled to room temperature or been frozen, I recommend reheating them for a few minutes in the microwave before serving. Refrigerator storage is not ideal since it dries muffins out quickly.

Muffins can be frozen for up to 2 weeks. If you plan on freezing them, do so right after they have cooled to room temperature. (They may become a bit stale even a few hours later.) To ensure that your muffins don't absorb freezer odors or get damaged by frost, wrap them individually in plastic cling wrap before storing in a plastic container and freezing.

TOOLS

Candy thermometer

An excellent tool for gauging the heat of liquids as they cook. If you have one, use it to test egg whites as they are whisked into the Swiss Meringue Buttercream Frosting and Seven-Minute Frosting, or when making sugar syrup for the Caramelized Popcorn.

Electric mixer

Ideal for creaming butter and sugar for cupcake batter.

Ice-cream scoop

For cupcakes and muffins with smooth dome-shaped tops, use this to scoop the batter into the baking cups before baking.

Muffin and cupcake pans

A standard cupcake pan has 12 cups, each of which has a 2¾-inch diameter and holds about ½ cup of batter. A standard muffin pan has 12 cups, each of which has a 3½-inch diameter and holds about 1 cup of batter. Cupcake pans can be used to make small muffins, which I often do when the muffins are particularly sweet or rich. Mini muffin/cupcake pans are also available. These often have 12 or 24 cups, each of which has a diameter of about 2 inches and holds about 2 tablespoons of batter.

Paper liners

Available in a wide range of sizes, shapes, and colors. Excellent for enhancing the appearance of your cupcakes or muffins, paper liners also help you remove them easily from the pan. And clean-up is a lot quicker. Your guests may prefer liners as an aid to holding and eating their cupcakes and muffins. Reusable silicone liners are available but can be difficult to clean.

Piping bag with tip

Used to pipe filling into cupcakes and frosting on top. If you don't have a piping bag, don't feel you need to run out and buy one. Squeeze bottles are adequate alternatives for filling, and frosting can be spread with a flat knife. You can also make your own bag by wrapping parchment paper into a cone shape and filling it with frosting, or by placing the frosting in a resealable plastic bag and making a small cut in one of the bottom corners.

Sifter

Used to combine dry ingredients such as flour, baking powder, and sugar. If you have one, use it, since it helps produce a more uniform batter and a cupcake with a lighter texture. Sifting doesn't take much effort, and the results are worth it.

INGREDIENTS

Butter

You'll notice that I use butter (not margarine) in many of these recipes since I find its taste and texture unrivaled. Note that some recipes call for melted butter, others for softened butter, and a few for cold butter. These distinctions are important. When creaming butter and sugar to make buttercream frosting and cupcakes, the butter should be softened but not melted, so that it forms a smooth cream when blended with sugar. When mixing butter with sugar to make muffins, the butter should be melted and brought to room temperature. When making streusel, the butter should be very cold so that it stays hard and forms crumbs. Once butter has been melted, it never regains its original texture.

Gel food coloring

Food coloring is used to tint icings, frostings, and batters. I recommend using gel food coloring since its colors are rich and full. It also provides a smooth, even color that isn't grainy.

Pasteurized egg whites

Several recipes in this book call for eggs that are not completely cooked. Though fresh eggs can be used in these recipes, they may be dangerous for children, the elderly, or anyone with a compromised immune system. In all cases, I recommend using liquid pasteurized eggs. Not only are they safer but they also eliminate waste since you won't be stuck with unused egg yolks.

Zests

Lemon, lime, and orange zest are natural flavorings that are excellent taste enhancers. When removing the zest from citrus fruit, be sure to stop before reaching the white membrane underneath. It is the outer, colored part that has flavor and aroma; the white inner layer is bitter.

Salt

Many recipes call for a pinch of salt. This is added to bring out sweetness and can be omitted if you like.

Metric Equivalents

The recipes that appear in this cookbook use the standard United States method for measuring liquid and dry or solid ingredients (teaspoons, tablespoons, and cups). The information on this chart is provided to help cooks outside the U.S. successfully use these recipes. All equivalents are approximate.

METRIC EQUIVALENTS FOR DIFFERENT TYPES OF INGREDIENTS

A standard cup measure of a dry or solid ingredient will vary in weight depending on the type of ingredient. A standard cup of liquid is the same volume for any type of liquid. Use the following chart when converting standard cup measures to grams (weight) or milliliters (volume).

Standard Cup	Fine Powder (ex. flour)	Grain (ex. rice)	Granular (ex. sugar)	Liquid Solids (ex. butter)	liquid (ex. milk)
1	140 g	150 g	190 g	200 g	240 ml
¾	105 g	113 g	143 g	150 g	180 ml
⅔	93 g	100 g	125 g	133 g	160 ml
½	70 g	75 g	95 g	100 g	120 ml
⅓	47 g	50 g	63 g	67 g	80 ml
¼	35 g	38 g	48 g	50 g	60 ml
⅛	18 g	19 g	24 g	25 g	30 ml

USEFUL EQUIVALENTS FOR DRY INGREDIENTS BY WEIGHT

(To convert ounces to grams, multiply the number of ounces by 30.)

1 oz	=	¹⁄₁₆ lb	=	30 g
4 oz	=	¼ lb	=	120 g
8 oz	=	½ lb	=	240 g
12 oz	=	¾ lb	=	360 g
16 oz	=	1 lb	=	480 g

USEFUL EQUIVALENTS FOR LENGTH

(To convert inches to centimeters, multiply the number of inches by 2.5.)

1 in				=	2.5 cm		
6 in	=	½ ft		=	15 cm		
12 in	=	1 ft		=	30 cm		
36 in	=	3 ft	=	1 yd	=	90 cm	
40 in				=	100 cm	=	1 m

USEFUL EQUIVALENTS FOR DRY INGREDIENTS BY WEIGHT

¼ tsp				=	1 ml
½ tsp				=	2 ml
1 tsp				=	5 ml
3 tsp	=	1 tbls		½ fl oz =	15 ml
		2 tbls =	⅛ cup	1 fl oz =	30 ml
		4 tbls =	¼ cup	2 fl oz =	60 ml
		5 ⅓ tbls =	⅓ cup	3 fl oz =	80 ml
		8 tbls =	½ cup	4 fl oz =	120 ml
		10 ⅔ tbls =	⅔ cup	5 fl oz =	160 ml
		12 tbls =	¾ cup	6 fl oz =	180 ml
		16 tbls =	1 cup	8 fl oz =	240 ml
		1 pt =	2 cups	16 fl oz =	480 ml
		1 qt =	4 cups	32 fl oz =	960 ml
			=	33 fl oz =	1000 ml = 1 liter

USEFUL EQUIVALENTS FOR COOKING/OVEN TEMPERATURES

	Fahrenheit	Celsius	Gas Mark
Freeze Water	32° F	0° C	
Room Temperature	68° F	20° C	
Boil Water	212° F	100° C	
Bake	325° F	160° C	3
	350° F	180° C	4
	375° F	190° C	5
	400° F	200° C	6
	425° F	220° C	7
	450° F	230° C	8
Broil			Grill

Index